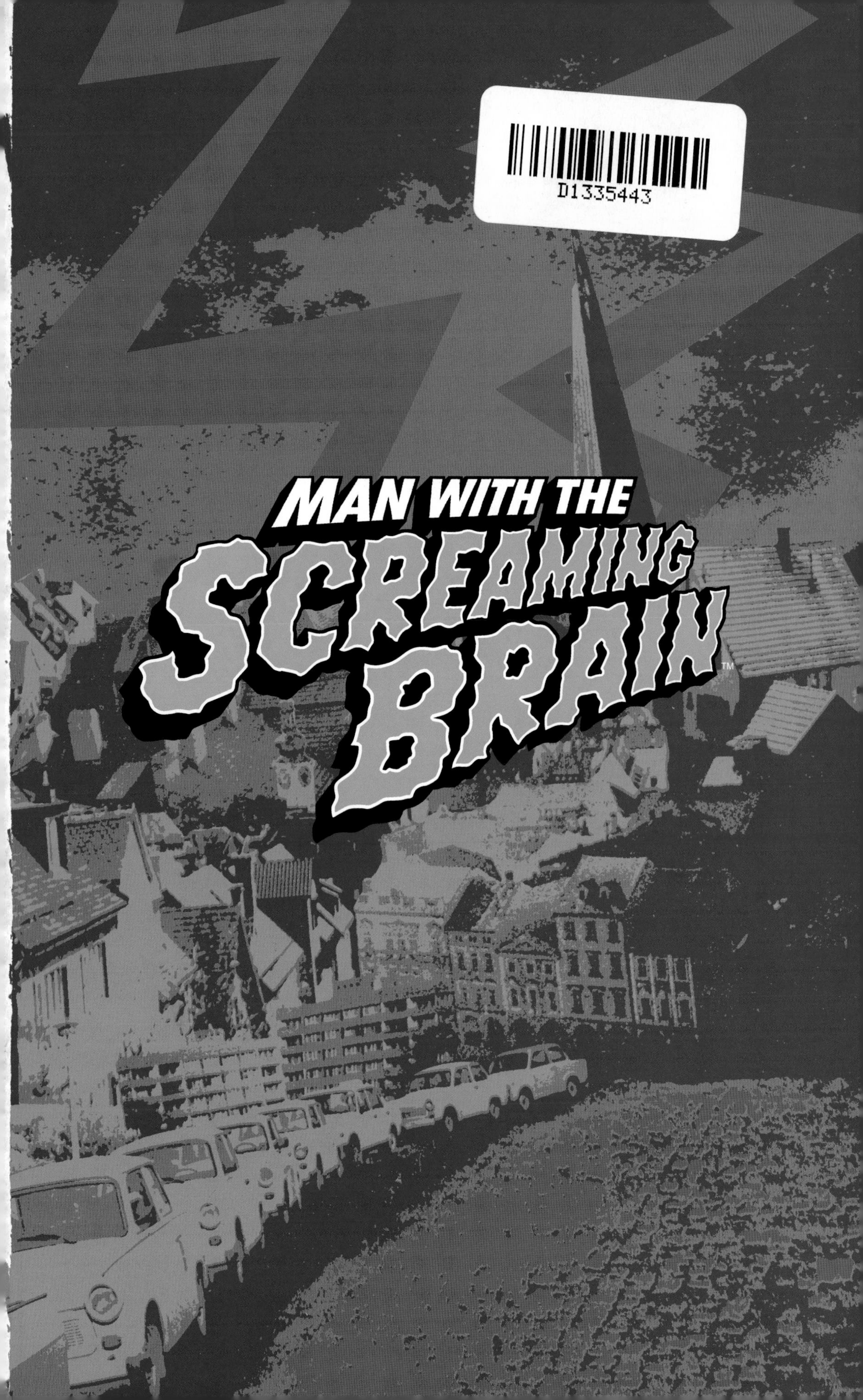
MAN WITH THE
SCREAMING
BRAIN™

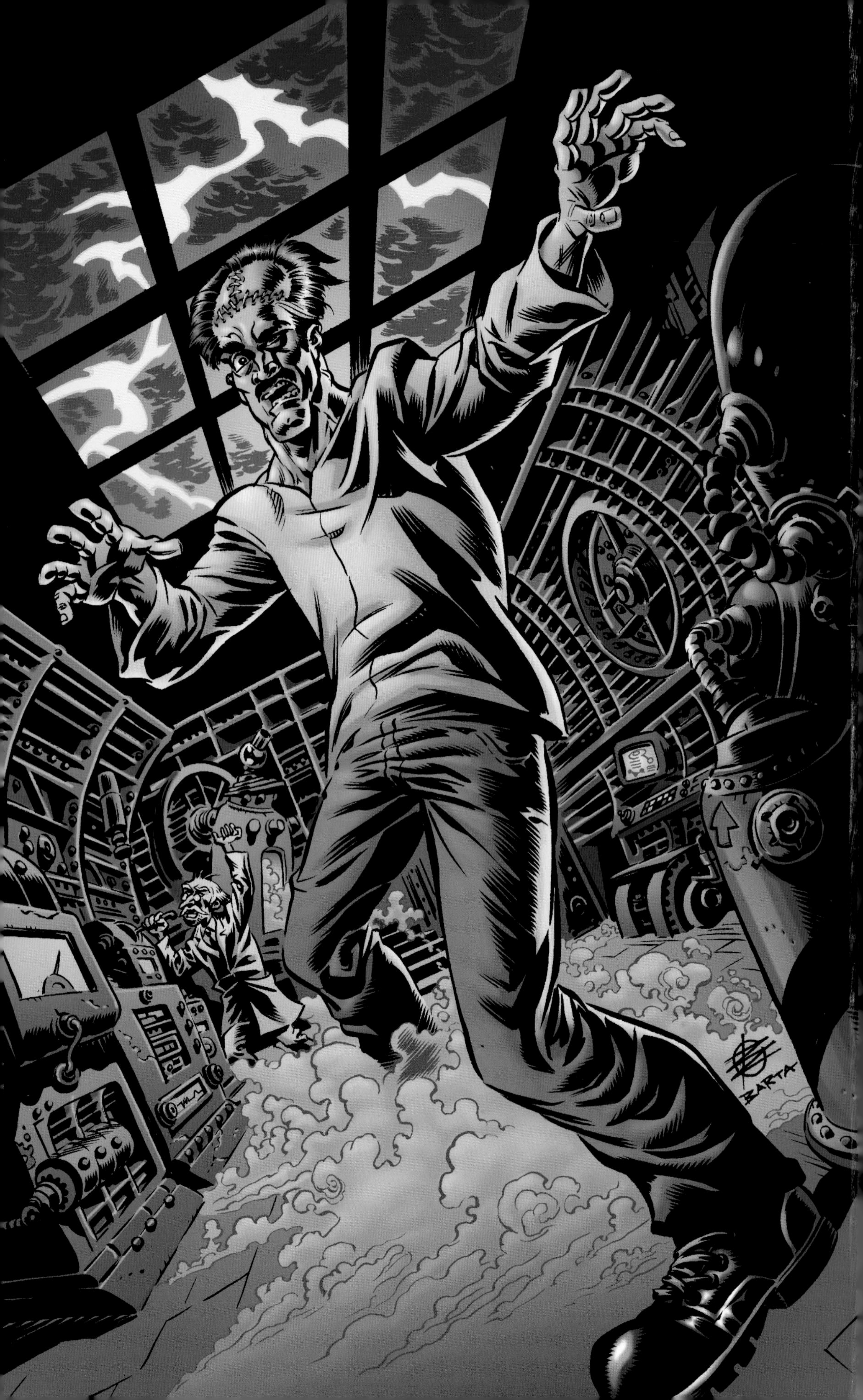
BARTA

MAN WITH THE SCREAMING BRAIN

STORY BY
BRUCE CAMPBELL AND **DAVID GOODMAN**

PENCILS BY
RICK REMENDER

FINISHES BY
HILARY BARTA

COLORS BY
MICHELLE MADSEN

LETTERS BY
NATE PIEKOS FOR **BLAMBOT**

BACKGROUND ASSISTS BY
CHRIS CARMEN

ADDITIONAL INKS BY
RANDY EMBERLIN

BASED ON THE MOTION PICTURE SCREENPLAY
MAN WITH THE SCREAMING BRAIN™ BY BRUCE CAMPBELL AND DAVID GOODMAN

DARK HORSE BOOKS™

PUBLISHER MIKE RICHARDSON

EDITOR SCOTT ALLIE

ASSISTANT EDITORS MATT DRYER AND DAVE MARSHALL

LOGO AND COLLECTION DESIGNER AMY ARENDTS

ART DIRECTOR LIA RIBACCHI

SPECIAL THANKS TO JASON HVAM, TODD HERMAN, AND GINA GAGLIANO

PUBLISHED BY
 DARK HORSE BOOKS
  A DIVISION OF DARK HORSE COMICS, INC.

DARK HORSE COMICS, INC.
 10956 SE MAIN STREET
  MILWAUKIE, OR 97222

WWW.DARKHORSE.COM

TO FIND A COMICS SHOP IN YOUR AREA,
 CALL THE COMIC SHOP LOCATOR SERVICE: 1-888-266-4226

FIRST EDITION: NOVEMBER 2005
 ISBN: 1-59307-397-6

10 9 8 7 6 5 4 3 2 1
PRINTED IN CHINA

THIS VOLUME COLLECTS ISSUES ONE THROUGH FOUR OF THE DARK HORSE COMIC-
 BOOK SERIES MAN WITH THE SCREAMING BRAIN.

HOW MUCH DO YOU TIP THE WHIPPER?

Since Bruce Campbell was too busy promoting his book and the movie (he's a shameless huckster when it comes to anything concerning himself—typical actor) my good friend Scott Allie called me to fill in exactly 2000 words about *Man with the Screaming Brain*.

"2001 words?" I asked.

"No, Goody, 2000," Scott replied.

"How about 1999?"

"No, Goody, 2000." Scott, like all great men of industry and science, clearly had a vision for this introduction.

"Okay," I said. "What should the point of this introduction be?"

"Oh, whatever's in your head."

"Well," I said. "There are a lot of things in my head. But who the heck cares what I have to say? I'm only the producer and writer. Which, come to think if it, reminds me of a joke. You ever hear the one about the Polish girl who went to Hollywood? She slept with the writer. Speaking of which, have you ever seen the German movie *Fitzcarraldo*? Well, if you haven't, it's about a lunatic who wants to take a steamship across land into the Amazon Jungle. You see, that's what it was like trying to get *Man with the Screaming Brain* made."

"That's nice," said Scott. "Can I get off the phone now?"

That's right, dear readers, believe it or not, it took eighteen years for *Man with the Screaming Brain* to finally see the light of day. Like an invincible abomination from another dimension, it was the movie that wouldn't die. And, trust me, there were plenty of times I wish it would have.

Over all those years, the story morphed into the movie and comic it is today (which, I should add, Bruce and I are mighty proud of). I don't want to bore you, but if you went through my file of cover letters regarding this movie, it would read like a living history of Hollywood in the eighties, nineties, and beyond. Many of the companies, with their letterhead so dignified and important looking, are now as dead as the dinosaurs.

Twice the film was set up (I have the *Variety* articles to prove it) and twice it fell apart, albeit for different reasons. The first time, Bruce got a television series just as we were scouting locations in Vancouver, and the second time, we didn't like the company we were dealing with.

With such a long development period, the script went through many incarnations. First there was a Hispanic version, and there was an Asian version when our foreign sales rep thought he could get a lot of money out of Japan. However, we ultimately ended up in Bulgaria.

Shooting over there came more out of necessity than any actual plan on our part. Which is another way of saying our Executive Producer, Jeff Franklin, who was putting up the money, told us we were going there.

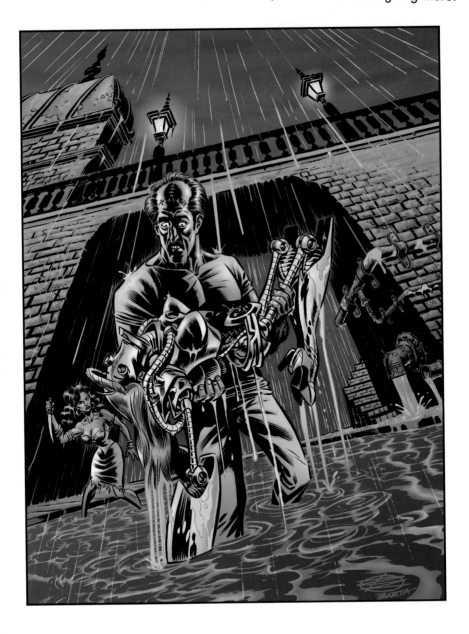

At first, Bruce and I were hesitant for a multitude of reasons, one being the war with Iraq, which just happens to be two countries away. Yet once we arrived, our insecurities quickly dissolved and we realized it was a great place.

Of course, making the film in Bulgaria required us to rewrite the script (again). Although the movie was originally set in America, we didn't have the money or resources to re-create the good ol' U.S. of A., so Bruce and I sat down and tried to figure out how to keep the essence of the story, yet make it work over there. Once we got started, we realized that setting it in an Eastern bloc country was quite helpful, because it furthered the "fish out of water" idea that was an essential structural device for the story. It created a twist I really liked—William Cole was as much a stranger in this country as he was inside his own body. Furthermore, since *Man with the Screaming Brain* is a riff on the Frankenstein story, the Eastern European setting really helped create the right atmosphere.

That said, we needed to figure out why Cole would be there in the first place. Luckily, my wife Alissa made me watch a *Frontline* documentary about American corporations going over to Europe to purchase public works as a corporate tax break. The minute I saw that, we had our reason.

Once all that was figured out, it wasn't too hard to turn all the Hispanic and Asian characters into Eastern Europeans. Oddly enough, what was hard was coming up with their names. It took quite a bit of time because each character had a distinct personality, so the name had to fit just right. Character names, like movie titles, are instinctual—they have to hit you in the gut or they don't work.

One other happy accident that came from shooting in Bulgaria was that it helped to set the style and tone of the comic. It allowed artists Rick Remender and Hilary Barta to really let loose their creative juices. Bruce and I had only one mandate for them: we wanted something in the vein of the EC comics of the 1950s. They both did a tremendous job and delivered more than we expected.

In a way, the screenplay lent itself perfectly to being a four-issue miniseries because it was eighty-nine pages long and most comics are twenty-two pages in length (4 x 22 = 88, for all you English majors). We didn't have to do much cutting and pasting with the script, and the boys knew exactly how to tailor it for the comics page.

A great idea of Scott's was to have guest artists do alternate covers on the book—although I don't think it was that hard of a sell, since many of the artists were fans of Bruce's work. I was really proud that so many really talented people wanted to work on something Bruce and I had created.

I know Bruce is really happy with the book, because it presents a truer vision of the story than the movie ever could. The comic captures a mood and tone that was impossible to achieve while making the picture due to time and budgetary constraints.

Yet, before we all start patting ourselves on the backs, some thanks are in order. Without the movie there would be no comic, and without Jeff Franklin (a true producer) and the SciFi Channel—particularly Thom Vitale—there would be no movie. They stayed involved over a long period of time, and through a lot of obstacles, because they really wanted to see this film get made.

What you learn in Hollywood if you stay here long enough is that most companies have the attention span of a fly. If your idea doesn't fit their particular profile at the moment, then off they go to the next thing. It's the producers and creators of projects who spend the long lonely nights trying to get their films made.

So if it's so hard, why do it? Why hold on to something for eighteen years, putting yourself through so much, emotionally and spiritually? It's not about money, even though that's what most people will tell you. The cash comes and goes. You do it because there are few things sweeter than seeing an idea you believe in come to fruition.

And sometimes you get really lucky, and you get to work with people like Mike Richardson and the crew at Dark Horse, who helped create this wonderful comic. I'll be honest with you—as much fun as you'll have reading *Man with the Screaming Brain*, it was more fun putting it together. The people behind this book are some of the most committed people I've ever had the pleasure of dealing with professionally. They do what they say, and more importantly, care about what they do. That's rare in this day and age.

—David Goodman
Los Angeles, California

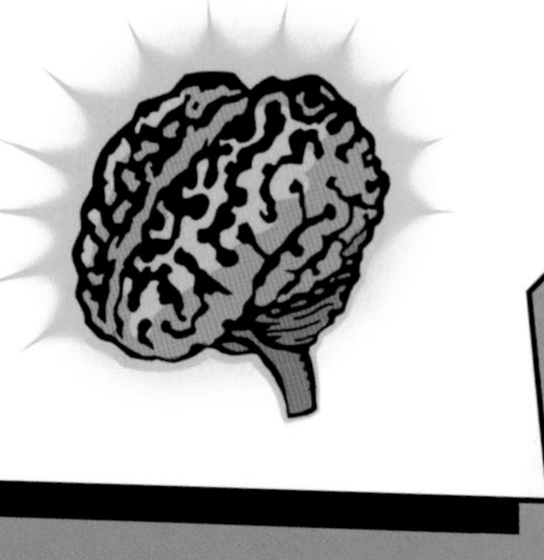

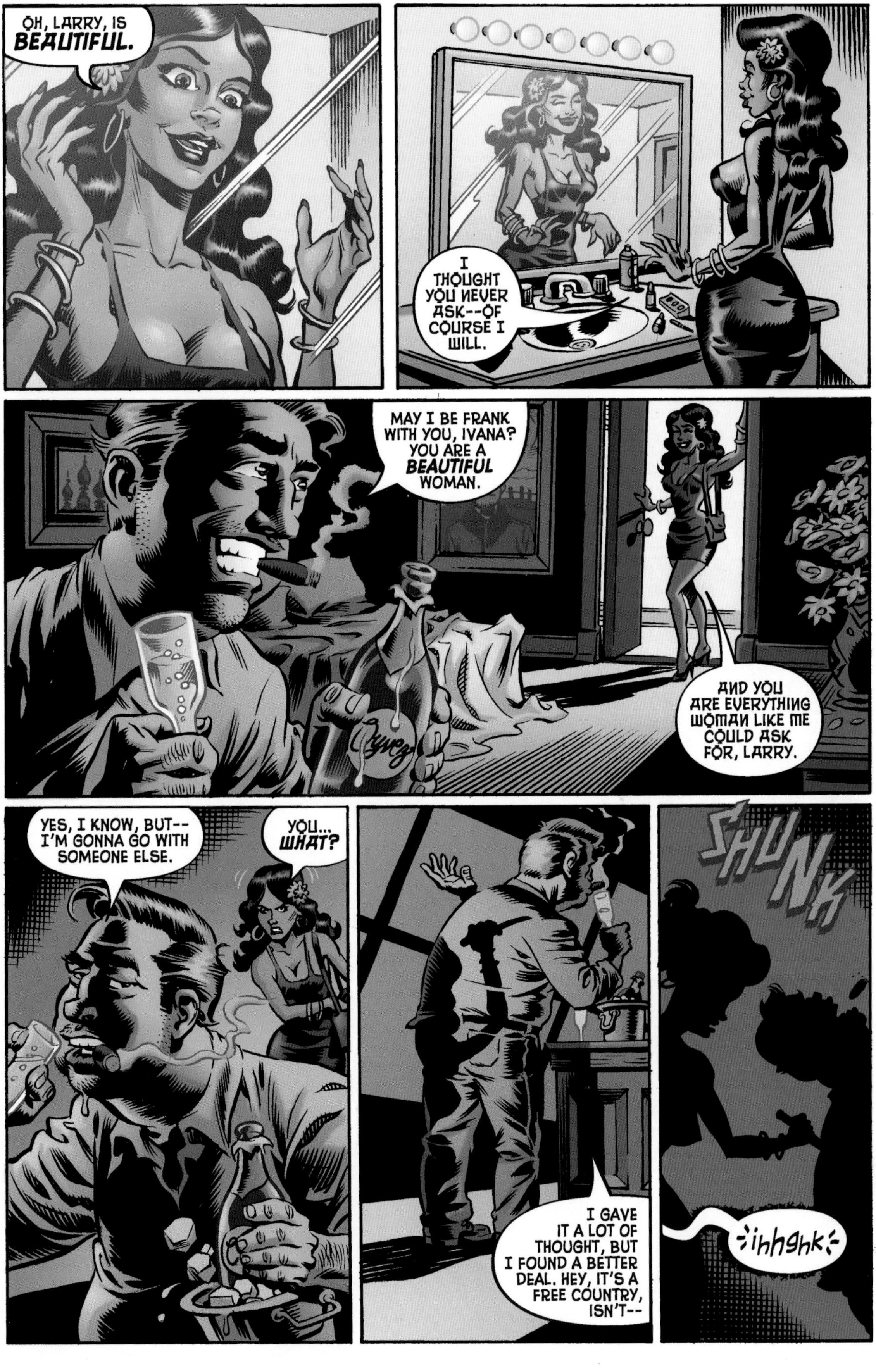

OH, LARRY, IS **BEAUTIFUL.**
I THOUGHT YOU NEVER ASK--OF COURSE I WILL.
MAY I BE FRANK WITH YOU, IVANA? YOU ARE A **BEAUTIFUL** WOMAN.
AND YOU ARE EVERYTHING WOMAN LIKE ME COULD ASK FOR, LARRY.
YES, I KNOW, BUT-- I'M GONNA GO WITH SOMEONE ELSE.
YOU... **WHAT?**
I GAVE IT A LOT OF THOUGHT, BUT I FOUND A BETTER DEAL. HEY, IT'S A FREE COUNTRY, ISN'T--
SHUNK
ihhghk

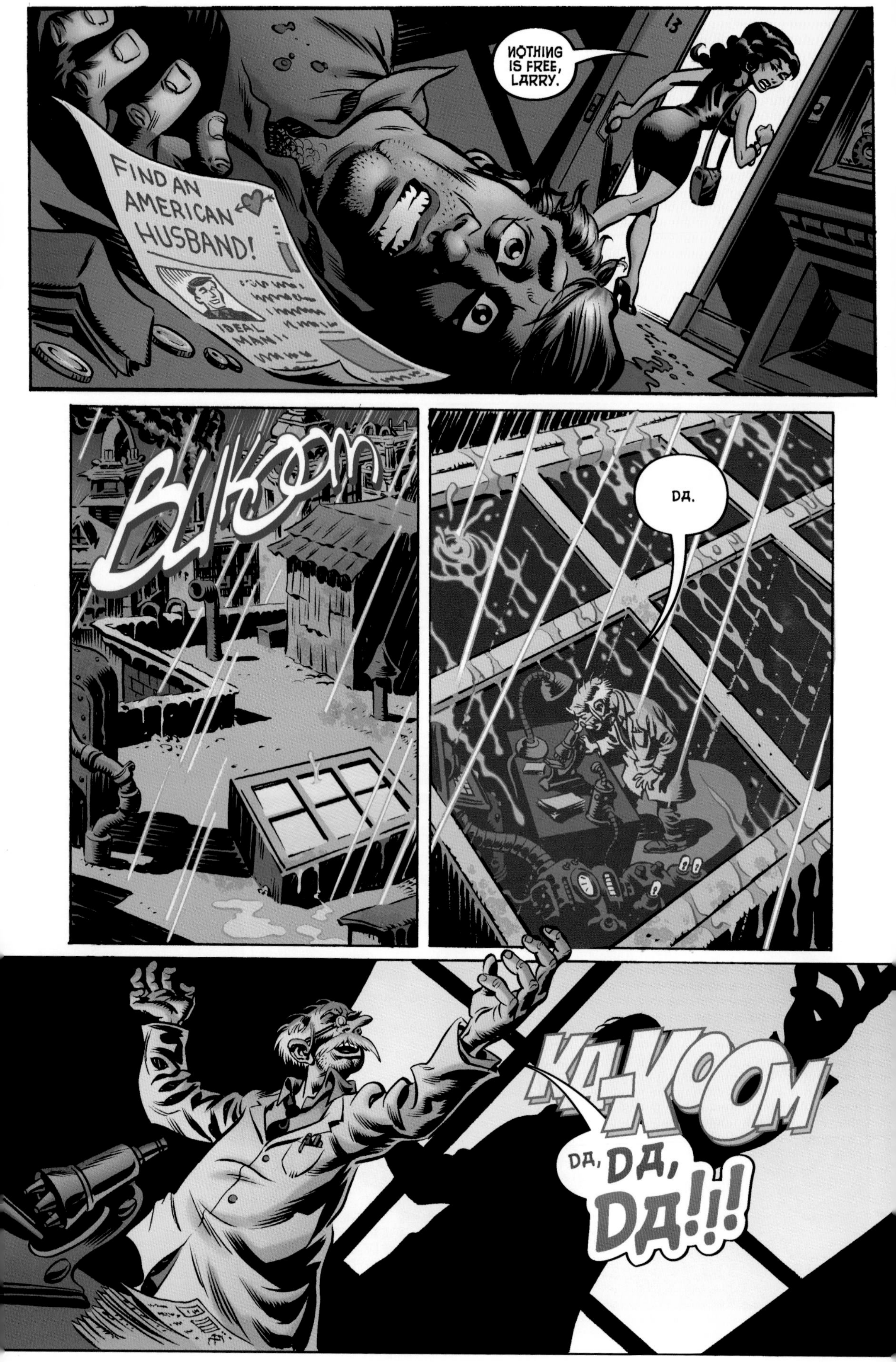
FIND AN AMERICAN HUSBAND!
IDEAL MAN!
NOTHING IS FREE, LARRY.
DA.
KA-KOOM
DA, DA, DA!!!

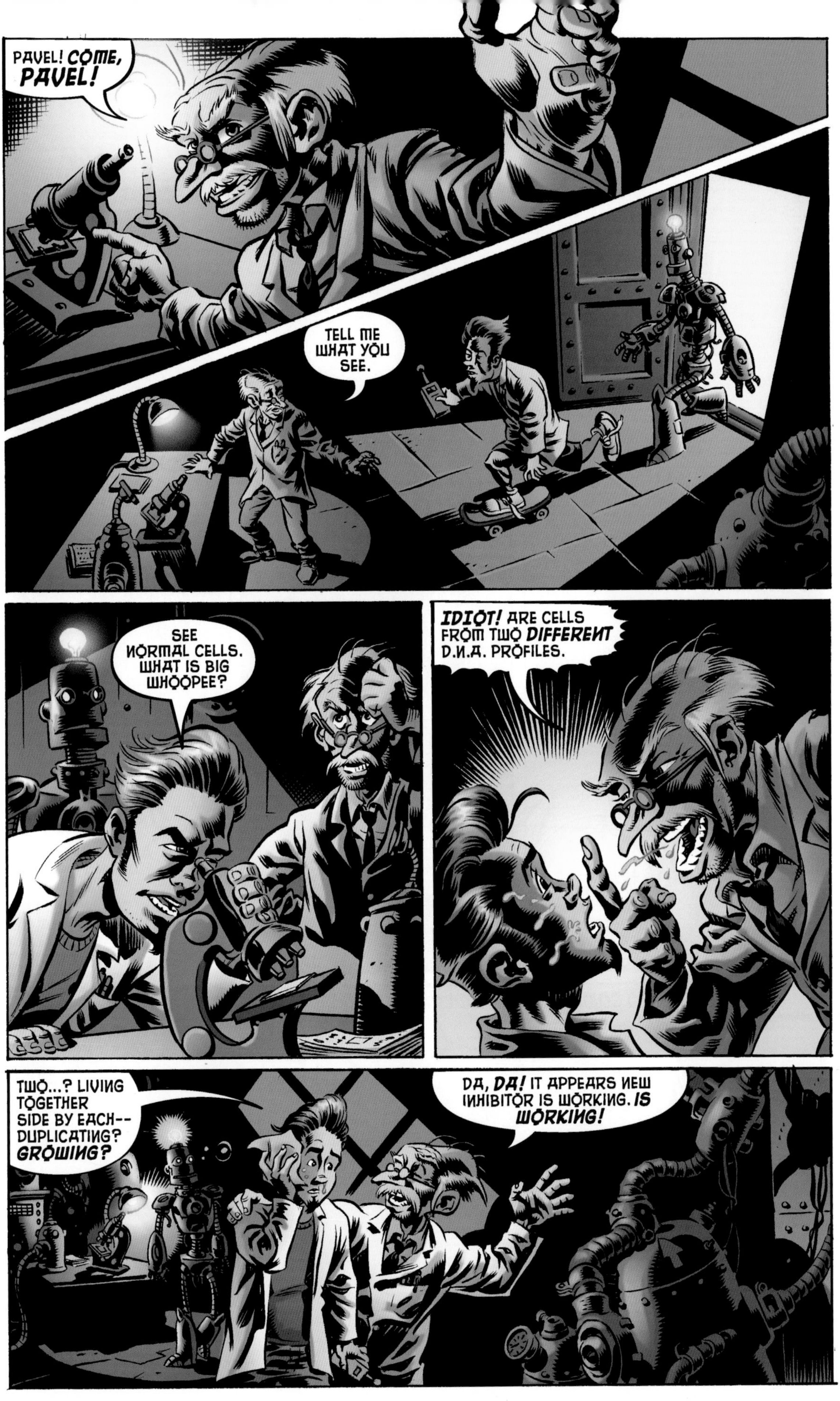
PAVEL! COME, PAVEL!
TELL ME WHAT YOU SEE.
SEE NORMAL CELLS. WHAT IS BIG WHOOPEE?
IDIOT! ARE CELLS FROM TWO DIFFERENT D.N.A. PROFILES.
TWO...? LIVING TOGETHER SIDE BY EACH-- DUPLICATING? GROWING?
DA, DA! IT APPEARS NEW INHIBITOR IS WORKING. IS WORKING!

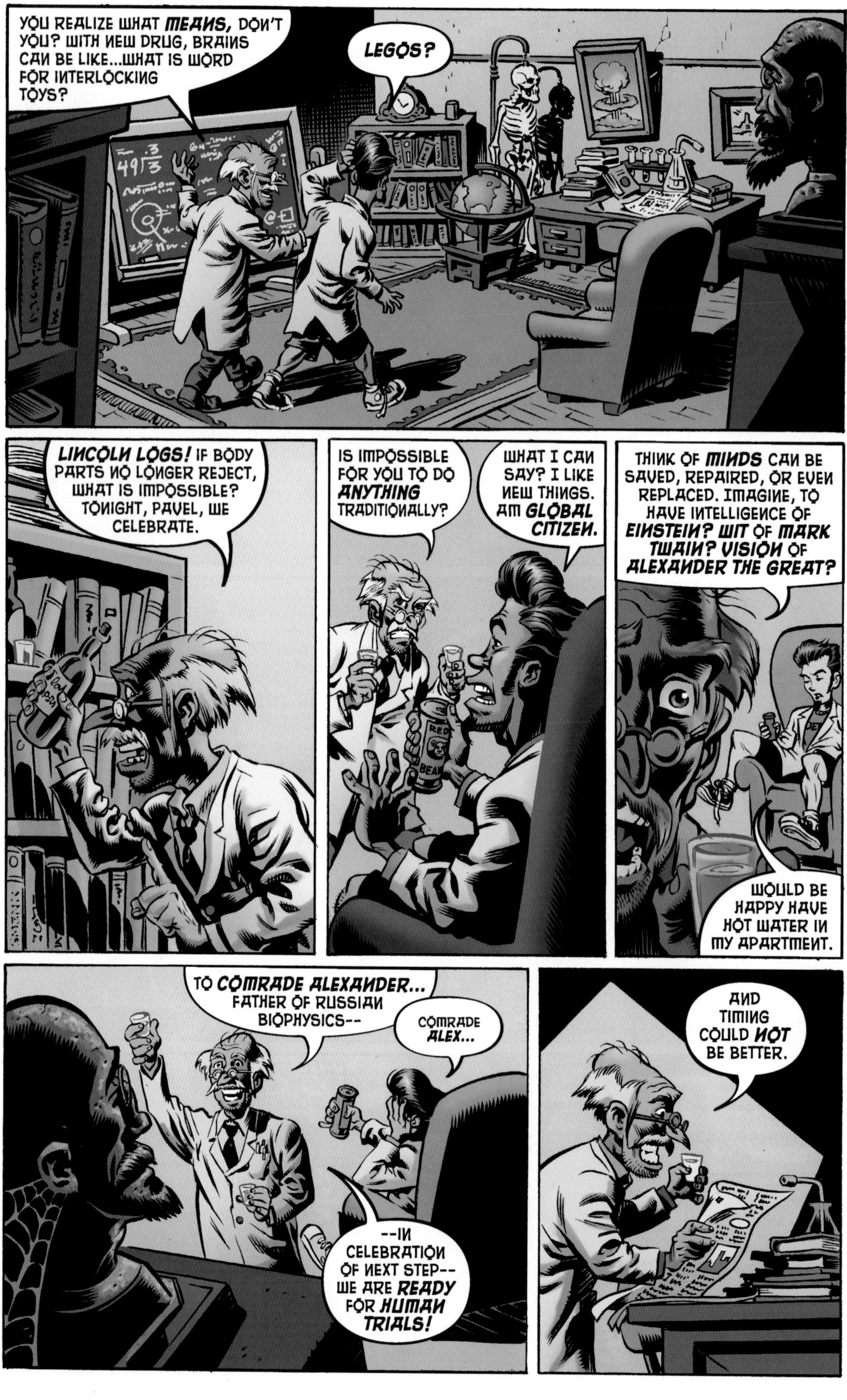
YOU REALIZE WHAT MEANS, DON'T YOU? WITH NEW DRUG, BRAINS CAN BE LIKE...WHAT IS WORD FOR INTERLOCKING TOYS?
LEGOS?
LINCOLN LOGS! IF BODY PARTS NO LONGER REJECT, WHAT IS IMPOSSIBLE? TONIGHT, PAVEL, WE CELEBRATE.
IS IMPOSSIBLE FOR YOU TO DO ANYTHING TRADITIONALLY?
WHAT I CAN SAY? I LIKE NEW THINGS. AM GLOBAL CITIZEN.
THINK OF MINDS CAN BE SAVED, REPAIRED, OR EVEN REPLACED. IMAGINE, TO HAVE INTELLIGENCE OF EINSTEIN? WIT OF MARK TWAIN? VISION OF ALEXANDER THE GREAT?
WOULD BE HAPPY HAVE HOT WATER IN MY APARTMENT.
TO COMRADE ALEXANDER... FATHER OF RUSSIAN BIOPHYSICS--
COMRADE ALEX...
--IN CELEBRATION OF NEXT STEP-- WE ARE READY FOR HUMAN TRIALS!
AND TIMING COULD NOT BE BETTER.

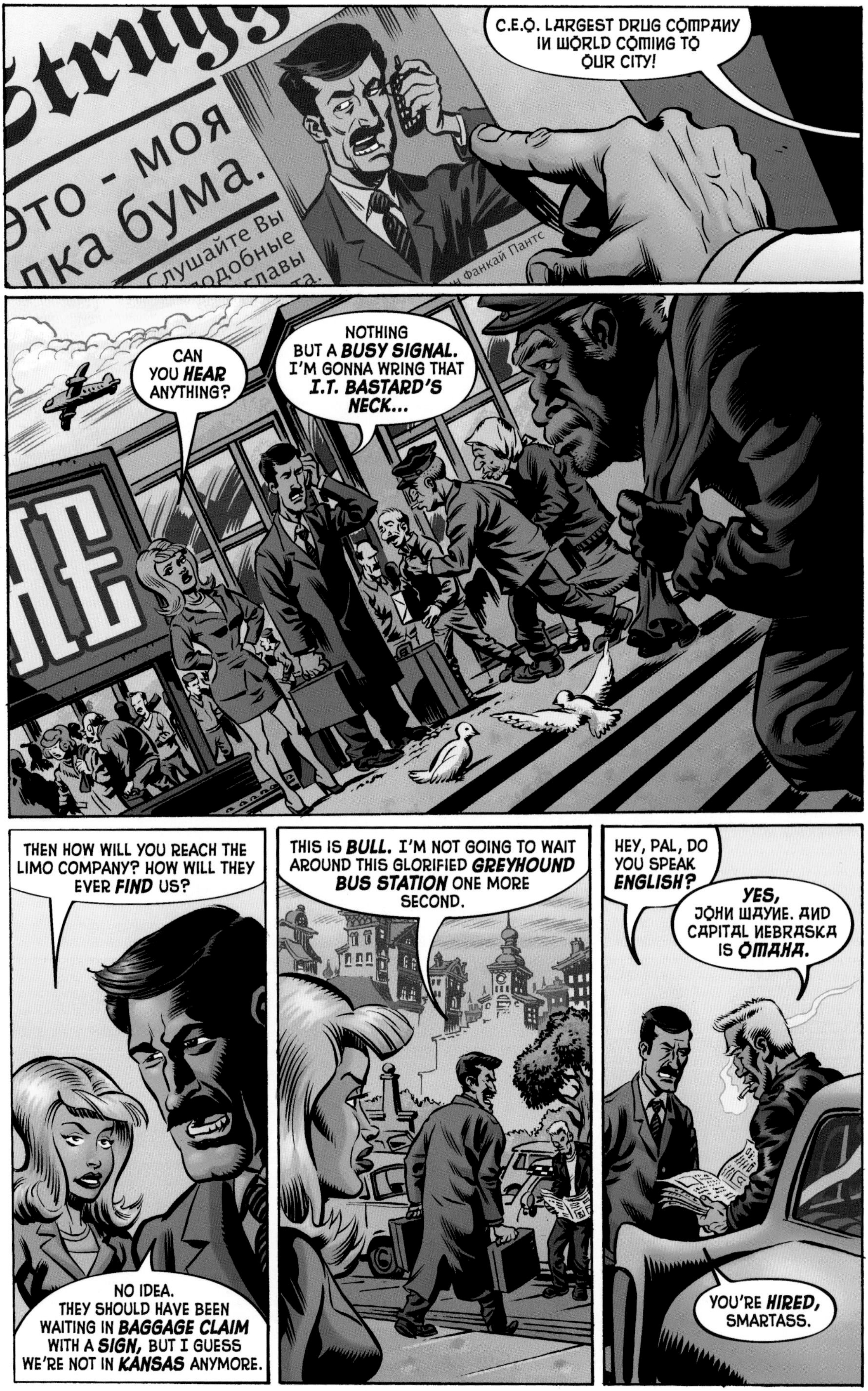
C.E.O. LARGEST DRUG COMPANY IN WORLD COMING TO OUR CITY!
CAN YOU HEAR ANYTHING?
NOTHING BUT A BUSY SIGNAL. I'M GONNA WRING THAT I.T. BASTARD'S NECK...
THEN HOW WILL YOU REACH THE LIMO COMPANY? HOW WILL THEY EVER FIND US?
NO IDEA. THEY SHOULD HAVE BEEN WAITING IN BAGGAGE CLAIM WITH A SIGN, BUT I GUESS WE'RE NOT IN KANSAS ANYMORE.
THIS IS BULL. I'M NOT GOING TO WAIT AROUND THIS GLORIFIED GREYHOUND BUS STATION ONE MORE SECOND.
HEY, PAL, DO YOU SPEAK ENGLISH?
YES, JOHN WAYNE. AND CAPITAL NEBRASKA IS OMAHA.
YOU'RE HIRED, SMARTASS.

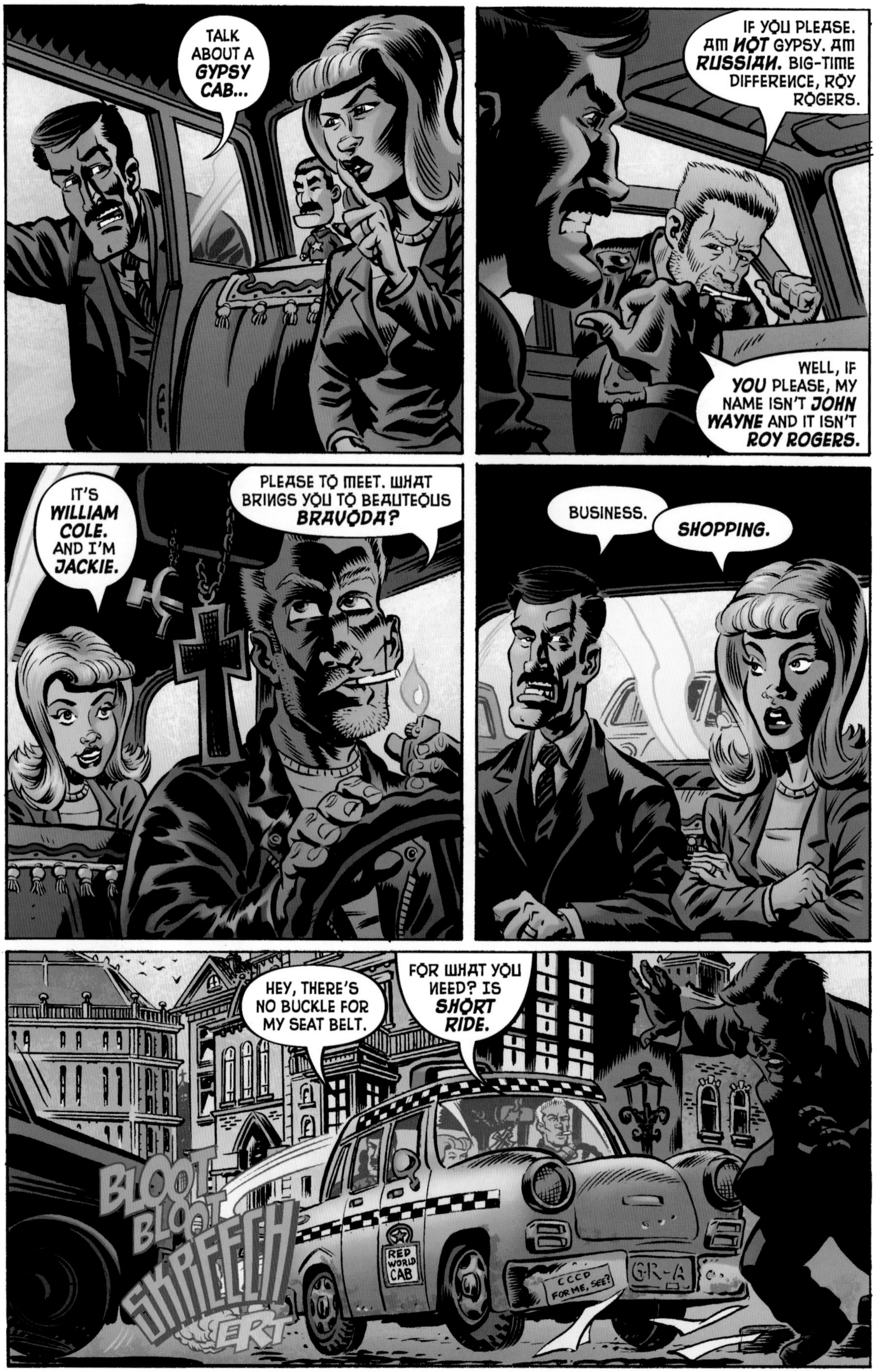
TALK ABOUT A GYPSY CAB...
IF YOU PLEASE. AM NOT GYPSY. AM RUSSIAN. BIG-TIME DIFFERENCE, ROY ROGERS.
WELL, IF YOU PLEASE, MY NAME ISN'T JOHN WAYNE AND IT ISN'T ROY ROGERS.
IT'S WILLIAM COLE. AND I'M JACKIE.
PLEASE TO MEET. WHAT BRINGS YOU TO BEAUTEOUS BRAVODA?
BUSINESS.
SHOPPING.
HEY, THERE'S NO BUCKLE FOR MY SEAT BELT.
FOR WHAT YOU NEED? IS SHORT RIDE.
BLOOT BLOOT
SKREECH
ERT
RED WORLD CAB
GR-A

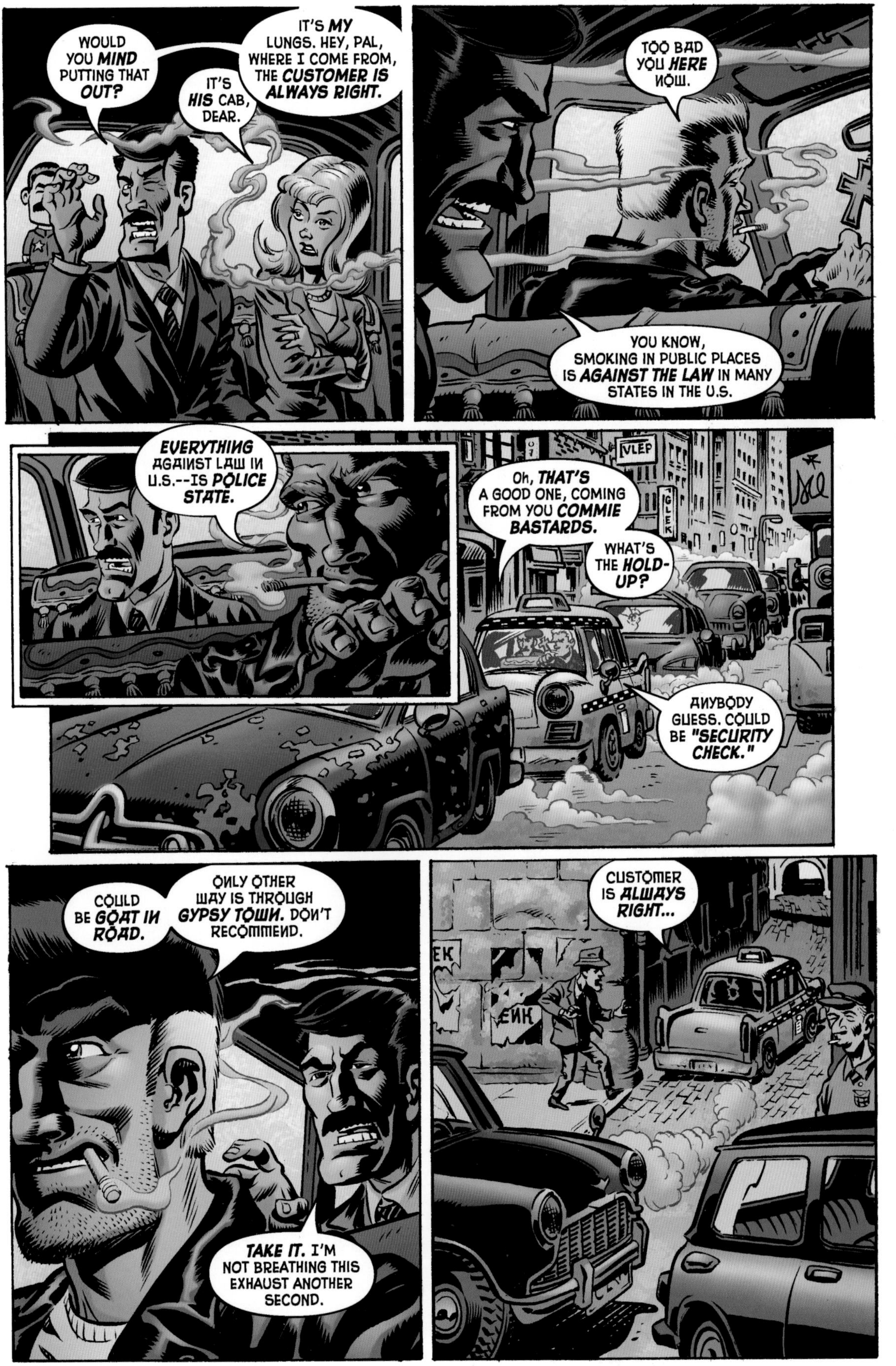
WOULD YOU MIND PUTTING THAT OUT?
IT'S MY LUNGS. HEY, PAL, WHERE I COME FROM, THE CUSTOMER IS ALWAYS RIGHT.
IT'S HIS CAB, DEAR.
TOO BAD YOU HERE NOW.
YOU KNOW, SMOKING IN PUBLIC PLACES IS AGAINST THE LAW IN MANY STATES IN THE U.S.
EVERYTHING AGAINST LAW IN U.S.--IS POLICE STATE.
VLEP
Oh, THAT'S A GOOD ONE, COMING FROM YOU COMMIE BASTARDS.
WHAT'S THE HOLD-UP?
ANYBODY GUESS. COULD BE "SECURITY CHECK."
COULD BE GOAT IN ROAD.
ONLY OTHER WAY IS THROUGH GYPSY TOWN. DON'T RECOMMEND.
TAKE IT. I'M NOT BREATHING THIS EXHAUST ANOTHER SECOND.
CUSTOMER IS ALWAYS RIGHT...

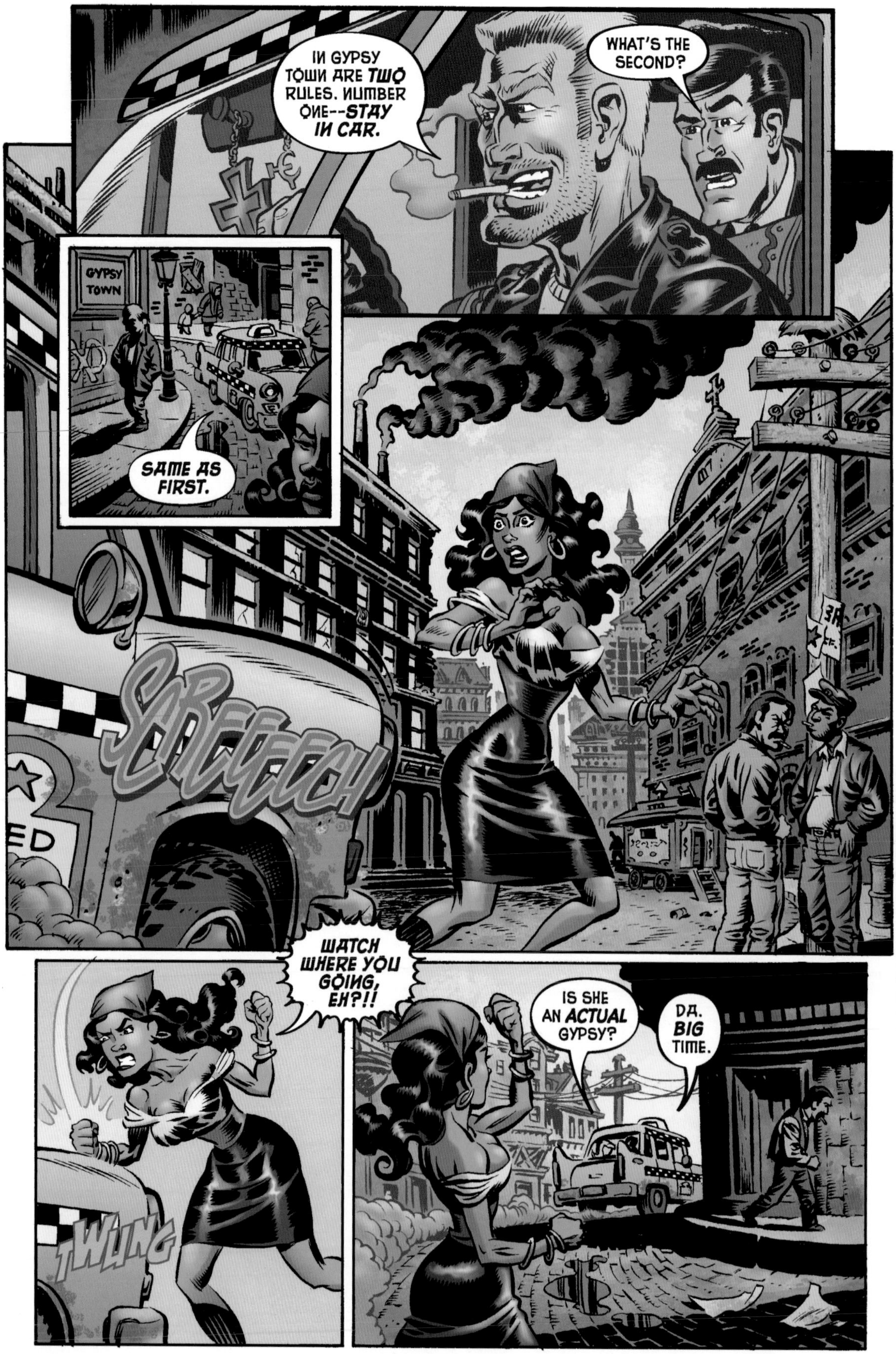
IN GYPSY TOWN ARE TWO RULES. NUMBER ONE--STAY IN CAR.
WHAT'S THE SECOND?
GYPSY TOWN
SAME AS FIRST.
SCREEECH
WATCH WHERE YOU GOING, EH?!!
TWUNG
IS SHE AN ACTUAL GYPSY?
DA. BIG TIME.

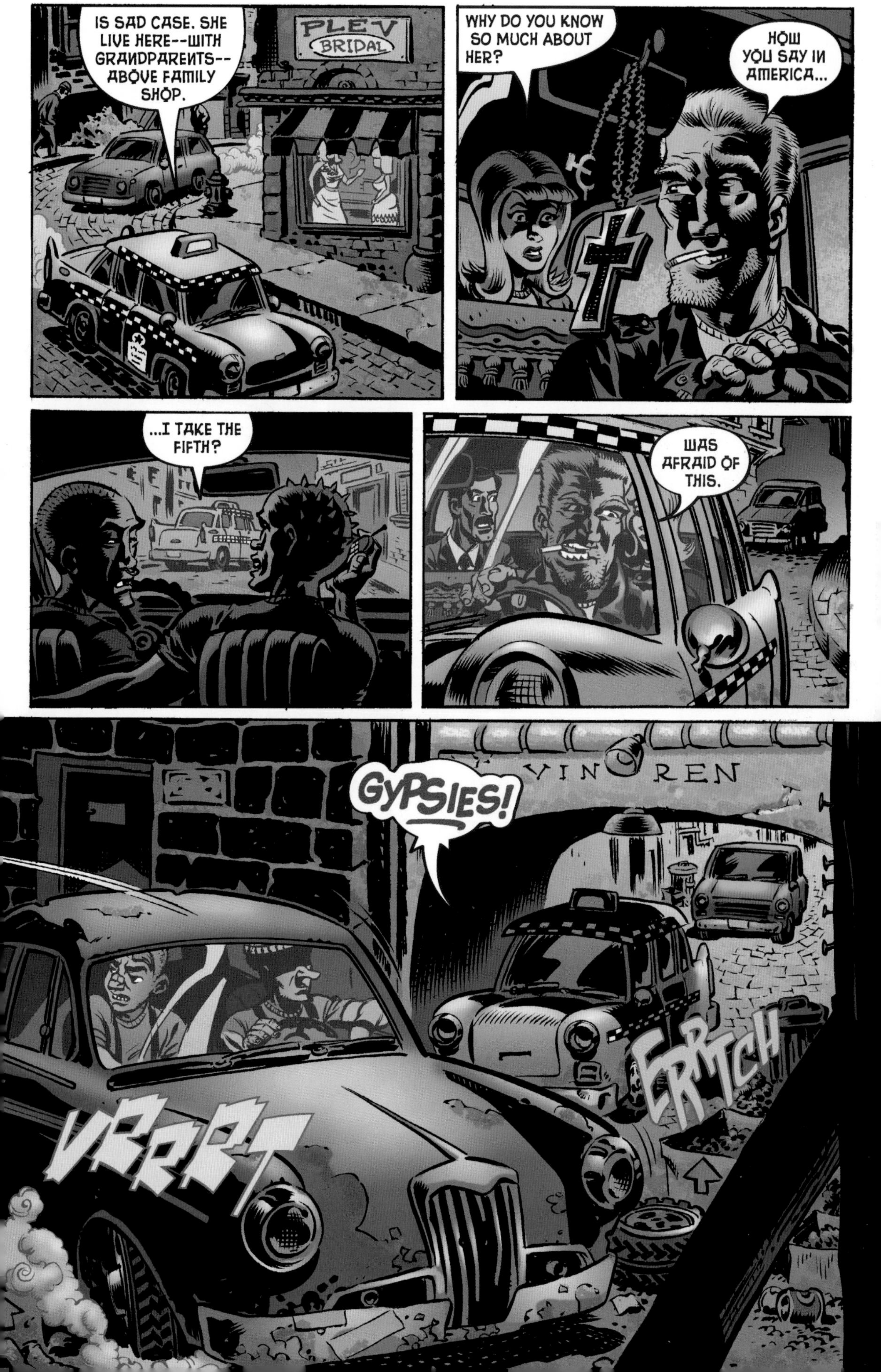
IS SAD CASE. SHE LIVE HERE--WITH GRANDPARENTS--ABOVE FAMILY SHOP.
PLEV
BRIDAL
WHY DO YOU KNOW SO MUCH ABOUT HER?
HOW YOU SAY IN AMERICA...
...I TAKE THE FIFTH?
WAS AFRAID OF THIS.
VIN REN
GYPSIES!
ERRTCH
VRRRT

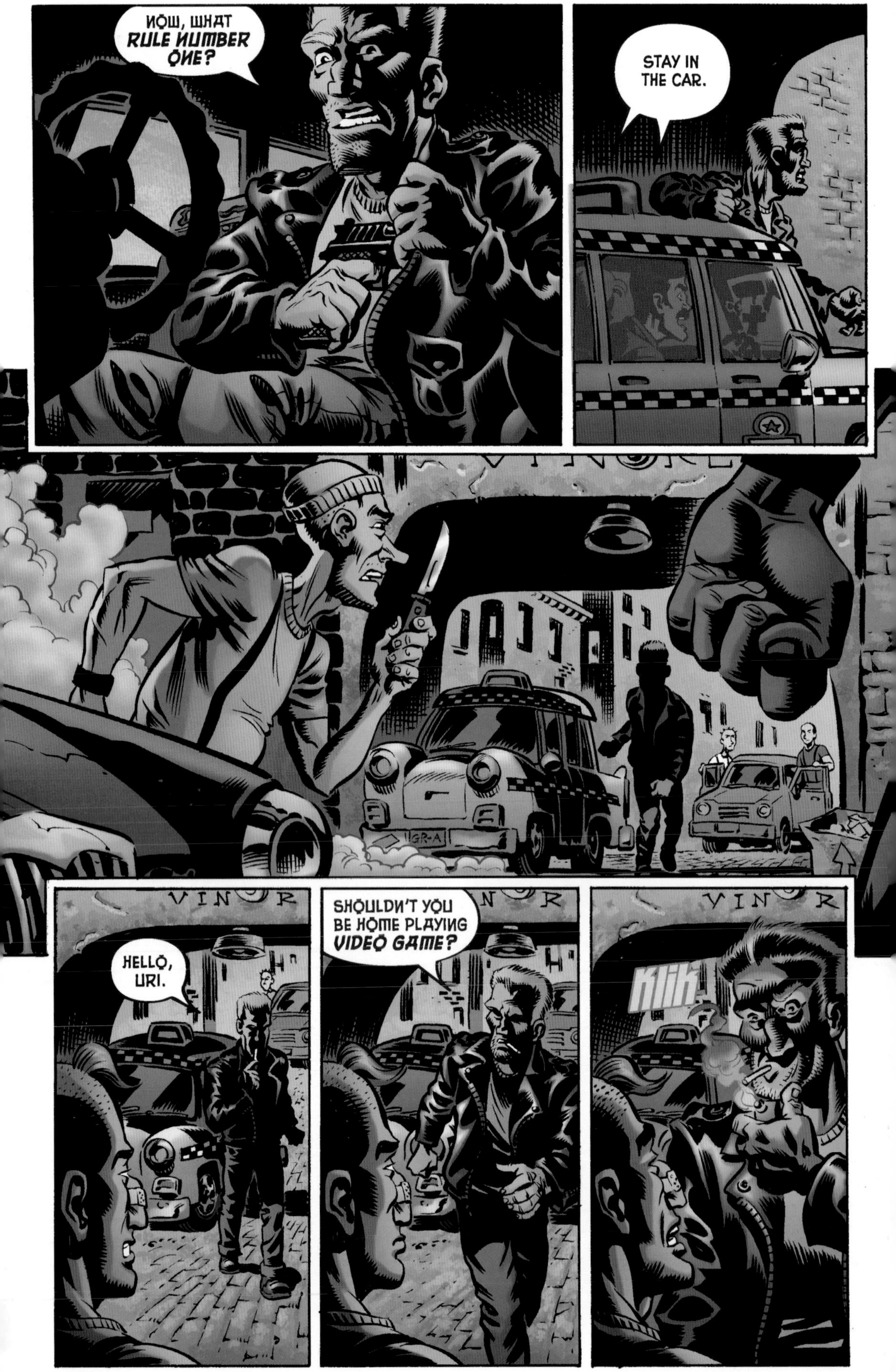
NOW, WHAT
RULE NUMBER
ONE?
STAY IN
THE CAR.
HELLO,
URI.
SHOULDN'T YOU
BE HOME PLAYING
VIDEO GAME?
KLIK!

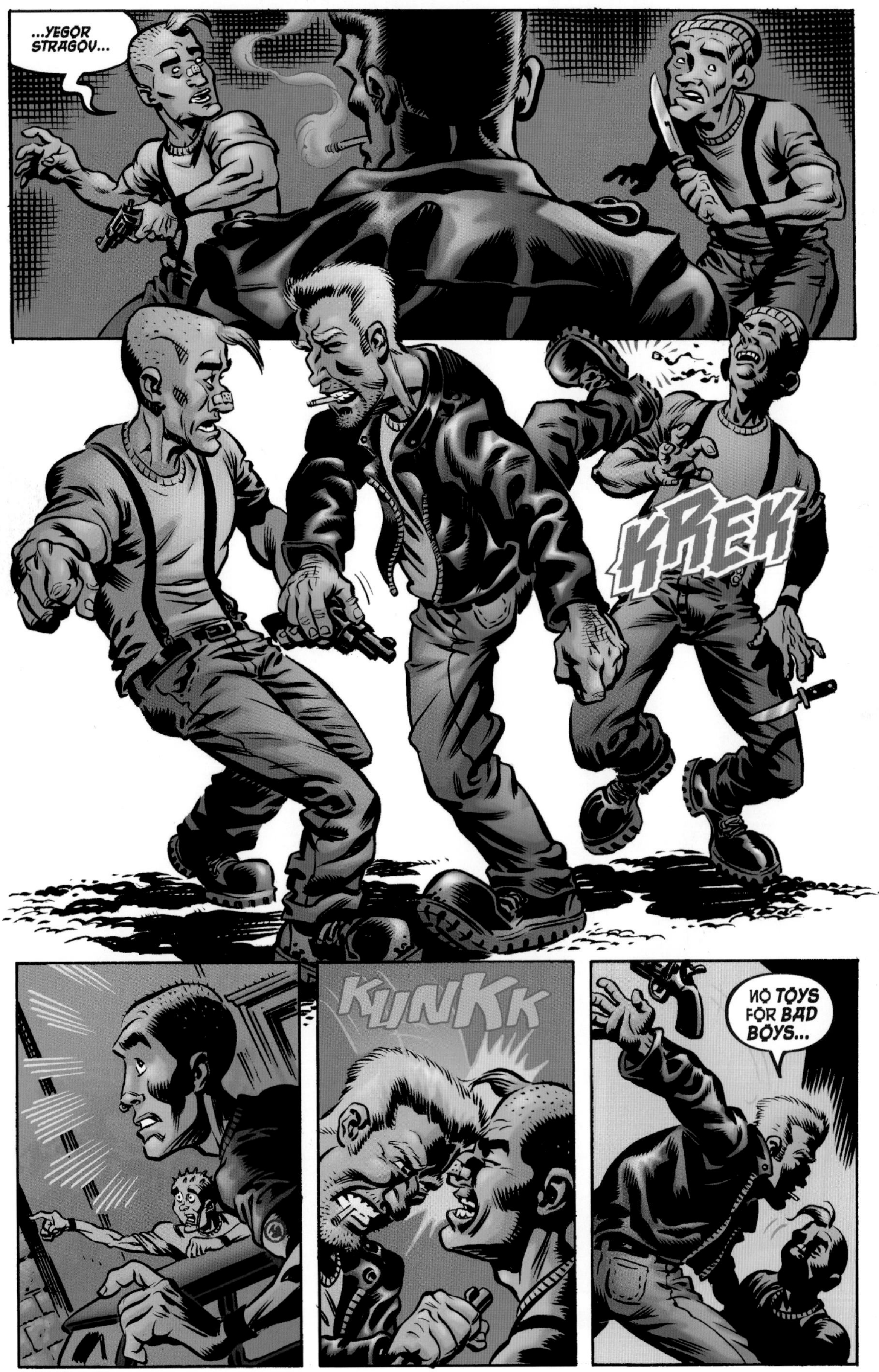

...YEGOR STRAGOV...
KREK
KLUNKK
NO TOYS FOR BAD BOYS...

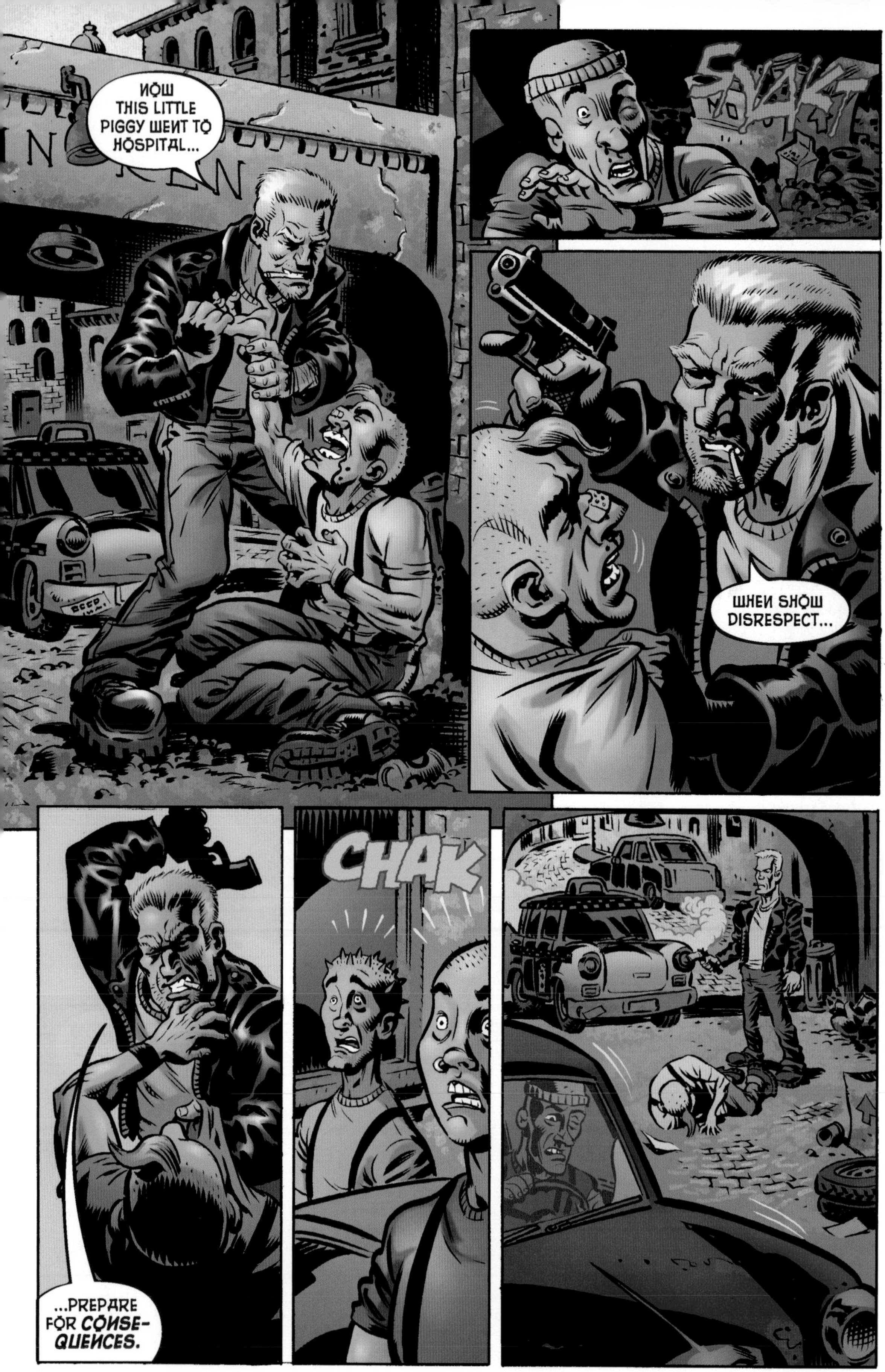
NOW THIS LITTLE PIGGY WENT TO HOSPITAL...
WHEN SHOW DISRESPECT...
...PREPARE FOR CONSE-QUENCES.
CHAK

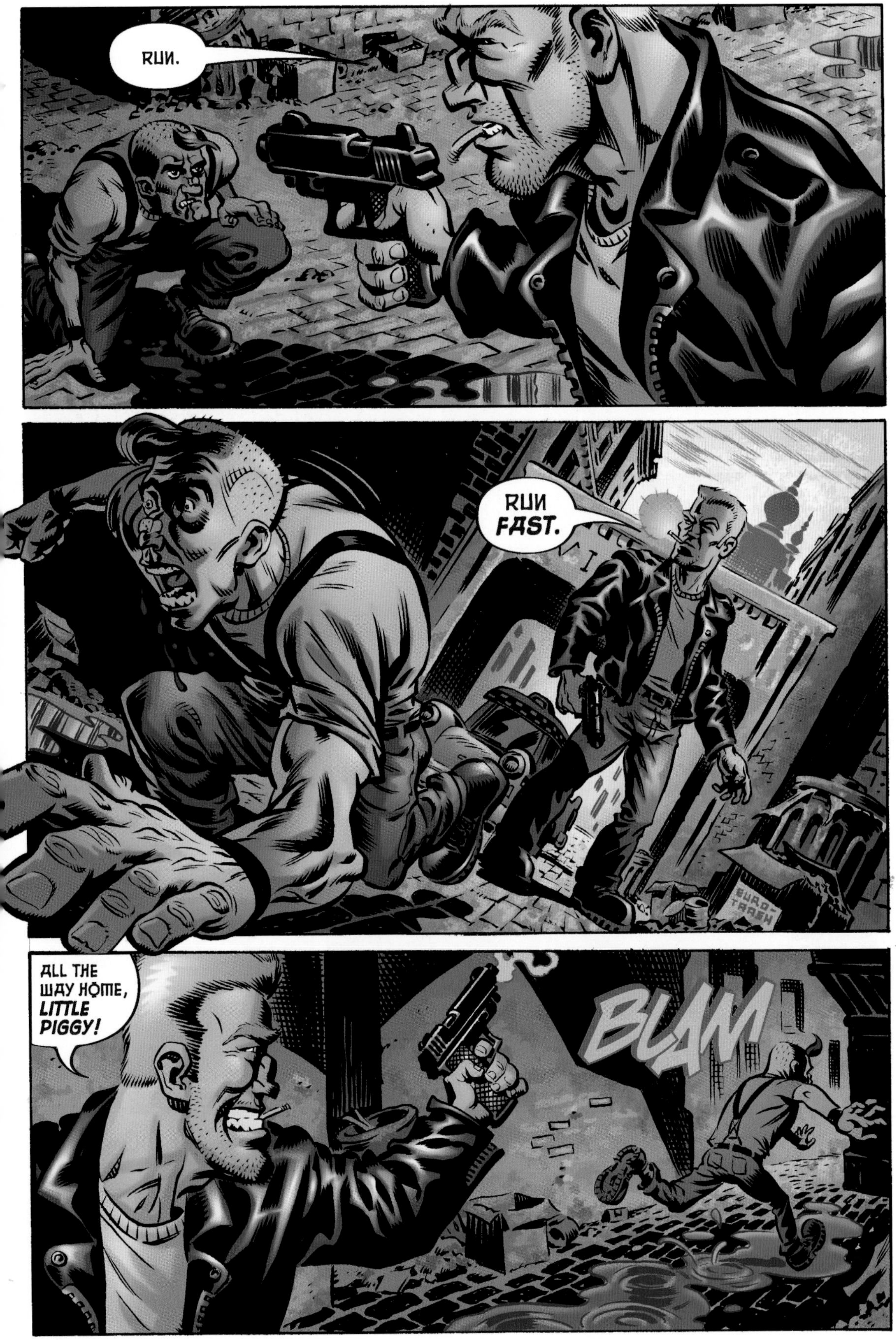
RUN.
RUN FAST.
ALL THE WAY HOME, LITTLE PIGGY!
BLAM
EURO-TRASH

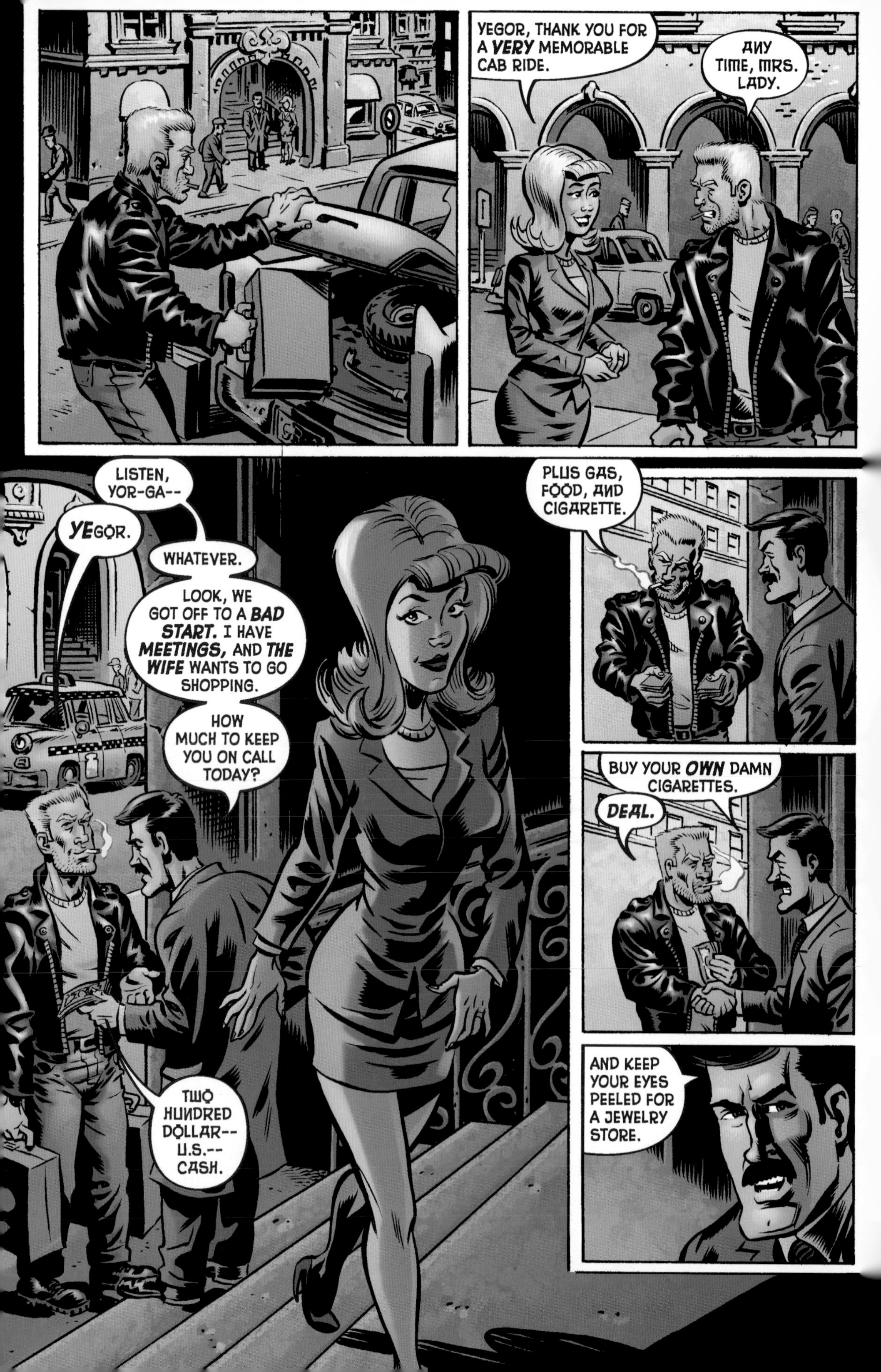
YEGOR, THANK YOU FOR A VERY MEMORABLE CAB RIDE.
ANY TIME, MRS. LADY.
LISTEN, YOR-GA--
YEGOR.
WHATEVER.
LOOK, WE GOT OFF TO A BAD START. I HAVE MEETINGS, AND THE WIFE WANTS TO GO SHOPPING.
HOW MUCH TO KEEP YOU ON CALL TODAY?
TWO HUNDRED DOLLAR-- U.S.-- CASH.
PLUS GAS, FOOD, AND CIGARETTE.
BUY YOUR OWN DAMN CIGARETTES.
DEAL.
AND KEEP YOUR EYES PEELED FOR A JEWELRY STORE.

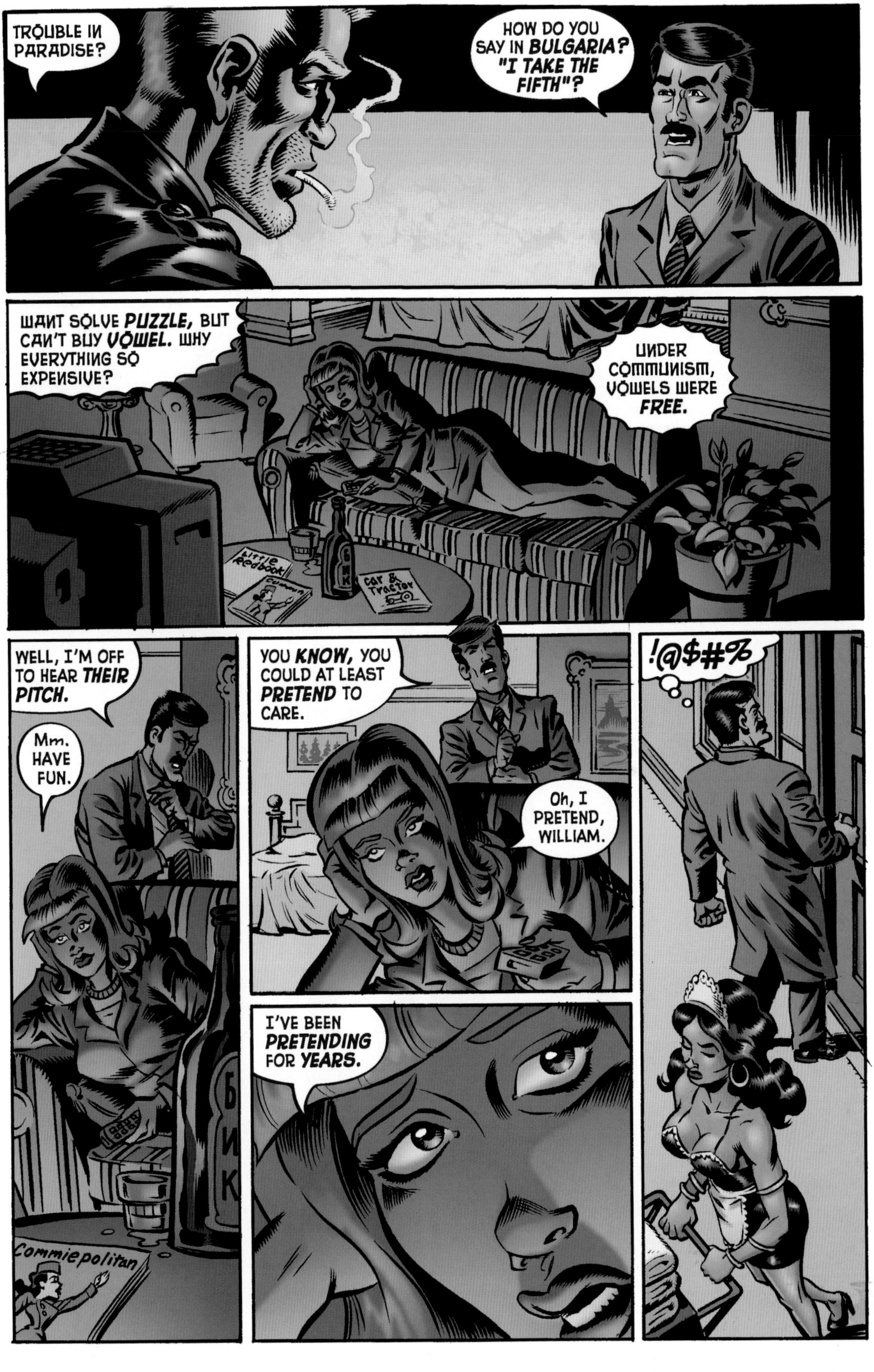
TROUBLE IN PARADISE?
HOW DO YOU SAY IN BULGARIA? "I TAKE THE FIFTH"?
WANT SOLVE PUZZLE, BUT CAN'T BUY VOWEL. WHY EVERYTHING SO EXPENSIVE?
UNDER COMMUNISM, VOWELS WERE FREE.
Little Redbook
Car & Tractor
WELL, I'M OFF TO HEAR THEIR PITCH.
Mm. HAVE FUN.
Commiepolitan
YOU KNOW, YOU COULD AT LEAST PRETEND TO CARE.
Oh, I PRETEND, WILLIAM.
I'VE BEEN PRETENDING FOR YEARS.
!@$#%

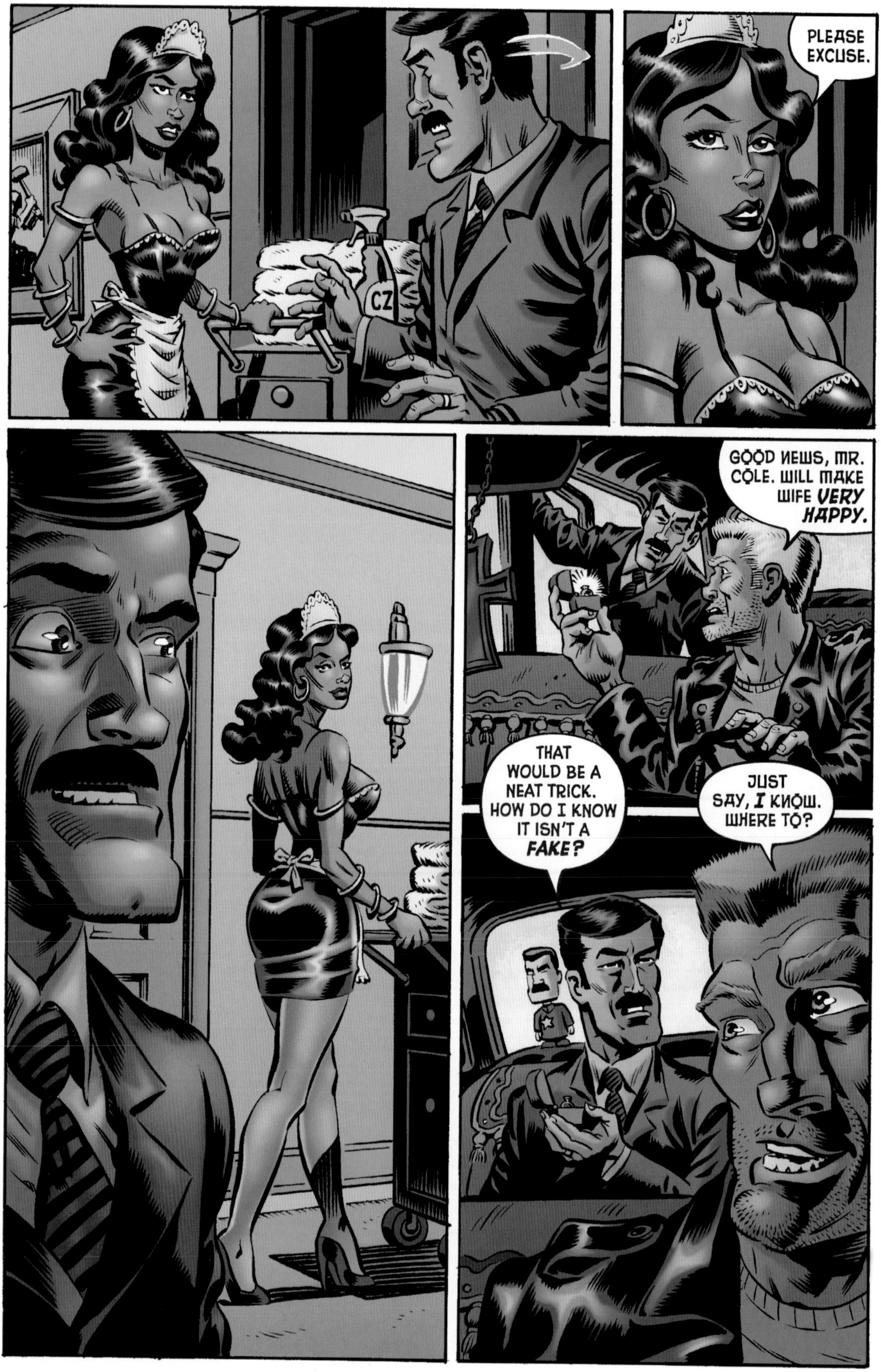
CZ
PLEASE EXCUSE.
GOOD NEWS, MR. COLE. WILL MAKE WIFE *VERY HAPPY.*
THAT WOULD BE A NEAT TRICK. HOW DO I KNOW IT ISN'T A *FAKE?*
JUST SAY, *I* KNOW. WHERE TO?

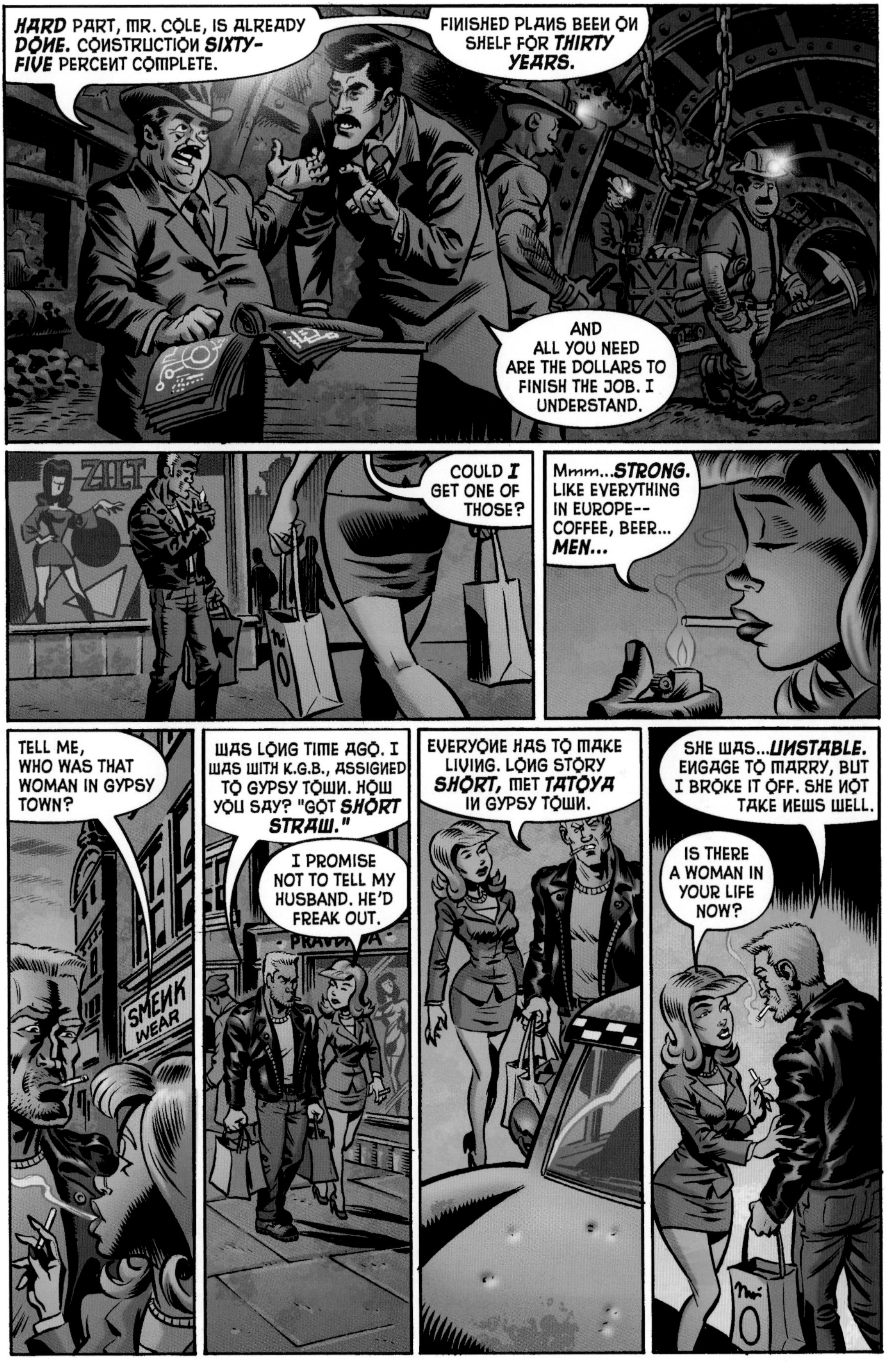

HARD PART, MR. COLE, IS ALREADY DONE. CONSTRUCTION SIXTY-FIVE PERCENT COMPLETE.
FINISHED PLANS BEEN ON SHELF FOR THIRTY YEARS.
AND ALL YOU NEED ARE THE DOLLARS TO FINISH THE JOB. I UNDERSTAND.
ZOLT
COULD I GET ONE OF THOSE?
Mmm...STRONG. LIKE EVERYTHING IN EUROPE--COFFEE, BEER... MEN...
TELL ME, WHO WAS THAT WOMAN IN GYPSY TOWN?
SMENK WEAR
WAS LONG TIME AGO. I WAS WITH K.G.B., ASSIGNED TO GYPSY TOWN. HOW YOU SAY? "GOT SHORT STRAW."
I PROMISE NOT TO TELL MY HUSBAND. HE'D FREAK OUT.
EVERYONE HAS TO MAKE LIVING. LONG STORY SHORT, MET TATOYA IN GYPSY TOWN.
SHE WAS...UNSTABLE. ENGAGE TO MARRY, BUT I BROKE IT OFF. SHE NOT TAKE NEWS WELL.
IS THERE A WOMAN IN YOUR LIFE NOW?

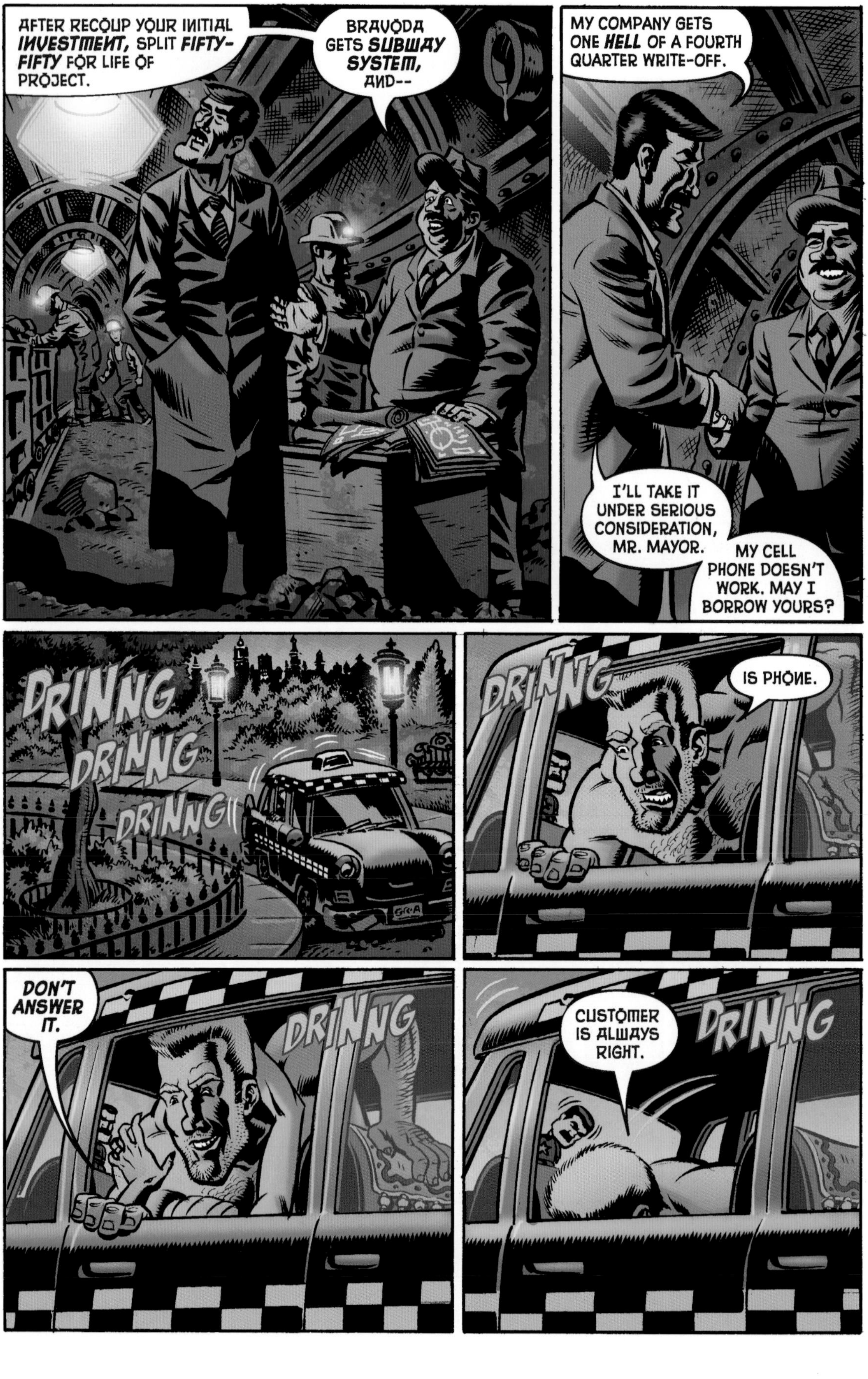
AFTER RECOUP YOUR INITIAL INVESTMENT, SPLIT FIFTY-FIFTY FOR LIFE OF PROJECT.
BRAVODA GETS SUBWAY SYSTEM, AND--
MY COMPANY GETS ONE HELL OF A FOURTH QUARTER WRITE-OFF.
I'LL TAKE IT UNDER SERIOUS CONSIDERATION, MR. MAYOR.
MY CELL PHONE DOESN'T WORK. MAY I BORROW YOURS?
DRINNG
DRINNG
DRINNG
DRINNG
IS PHONE.
DON'T ANSWER IT.
DRINNG
CUSTOMER IS ALWAYS RIGHT.
DRINNG

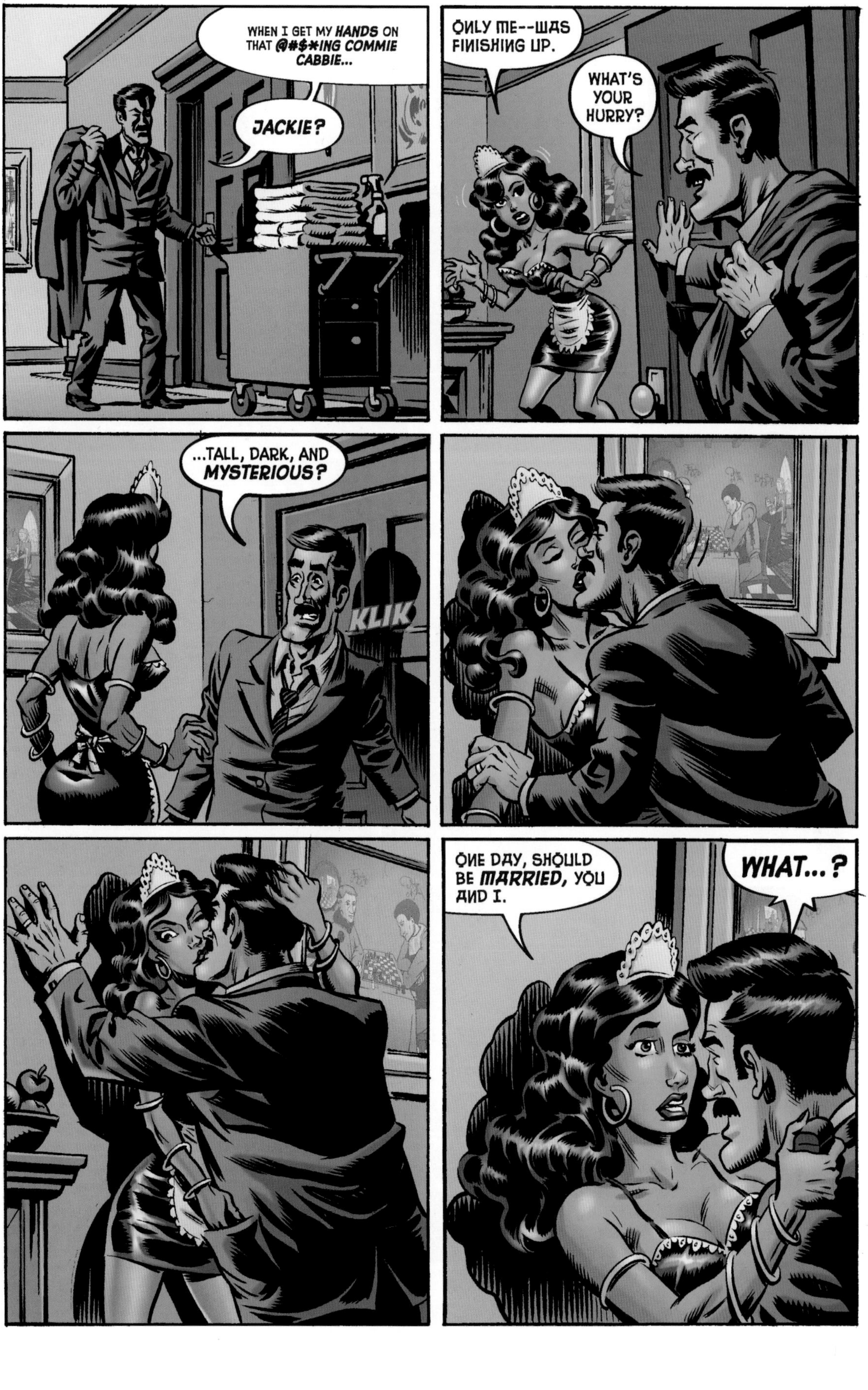
WHEN I GET MY HANDS ON THAT @#$*ING COMMIE CABBIE...
JACKIE?
ONLY ME--WAS FINISHING UP.
WHAT'S YOUR HURRY?
...TALL, DARK, AND MYSTERIOUS?
KLIK
ONE DAY, SHOULD BE MARRIED, YOU AND I.
WHAT...?

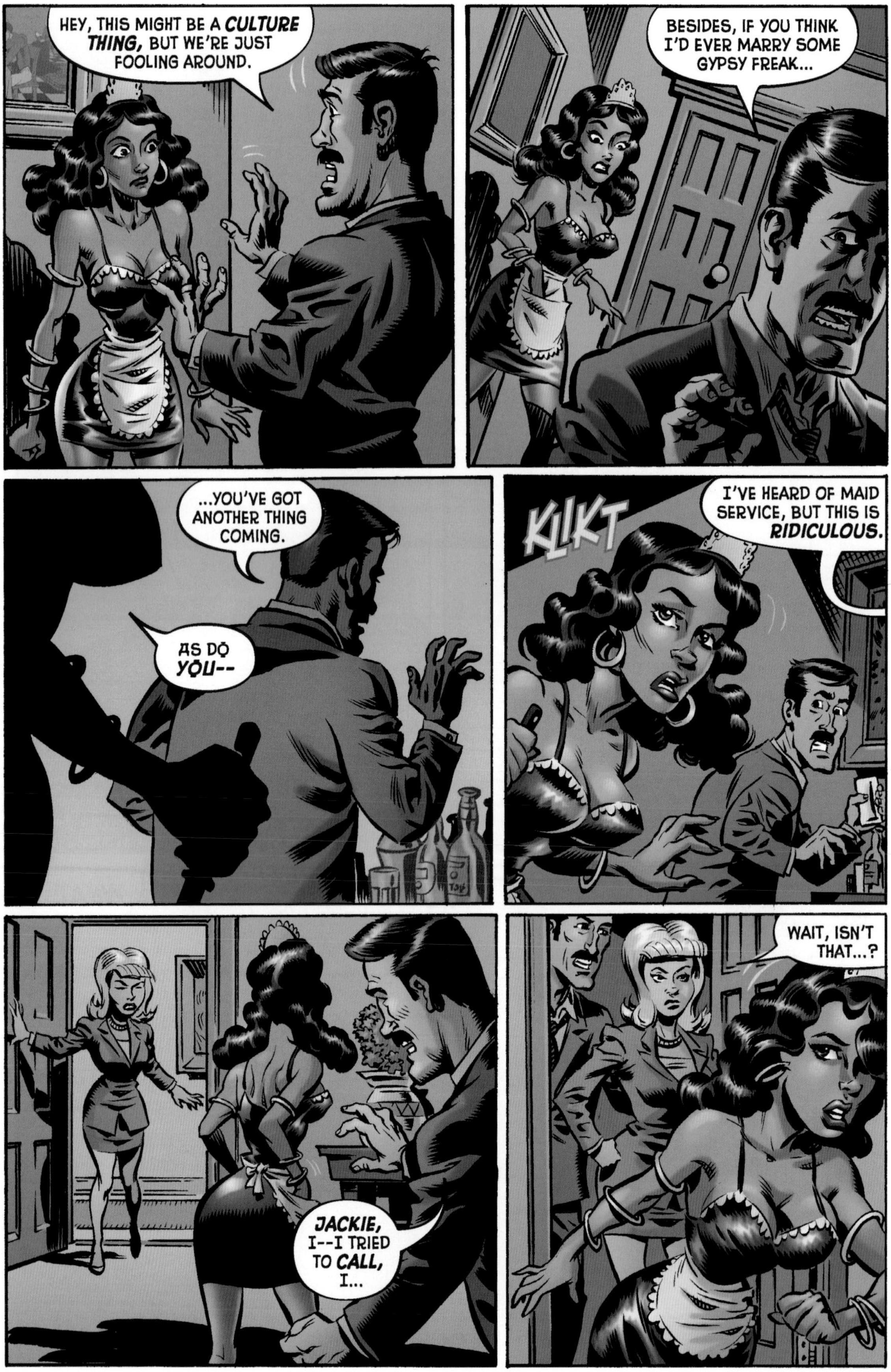
HEY, THIS MIGHT BE A *CULTURE THING,* BUT WE'RE JUST FOOLING AROUND.
BESIDES, IF YOU THINK I'D EVER MARRY SOME GYPSY FREAK...
...YOU'VE GOT ANOTHER THING COMING.
AS DO *YOU*--
KLIKT
I'VE HEARD OF MAID SERVICE, BUT THIS IS *RIDICULOUS.*
JACKIE, I--I TRIED TO *CALL,* I...
WAIT, ISN'T THAT...?

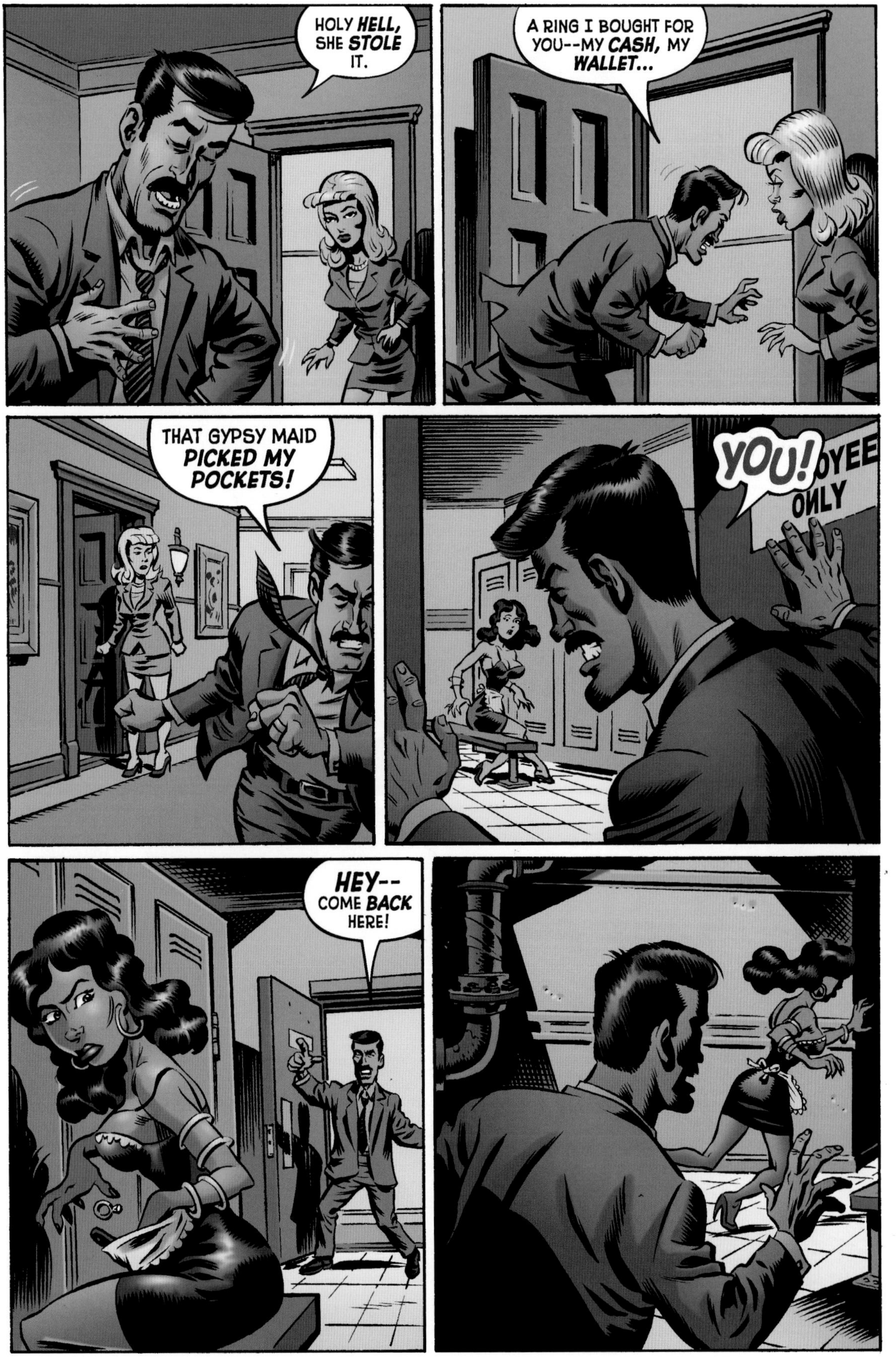
HOLY HELL, SHE STOLE IT.
A RING I BOUGHT FOR YOU--MY CASH, MY WALLET...
THAT GYPSY MAID PICKED MY POCKETS!
YOU!
OYEE ONLY
HEY--COME BACK HERE!

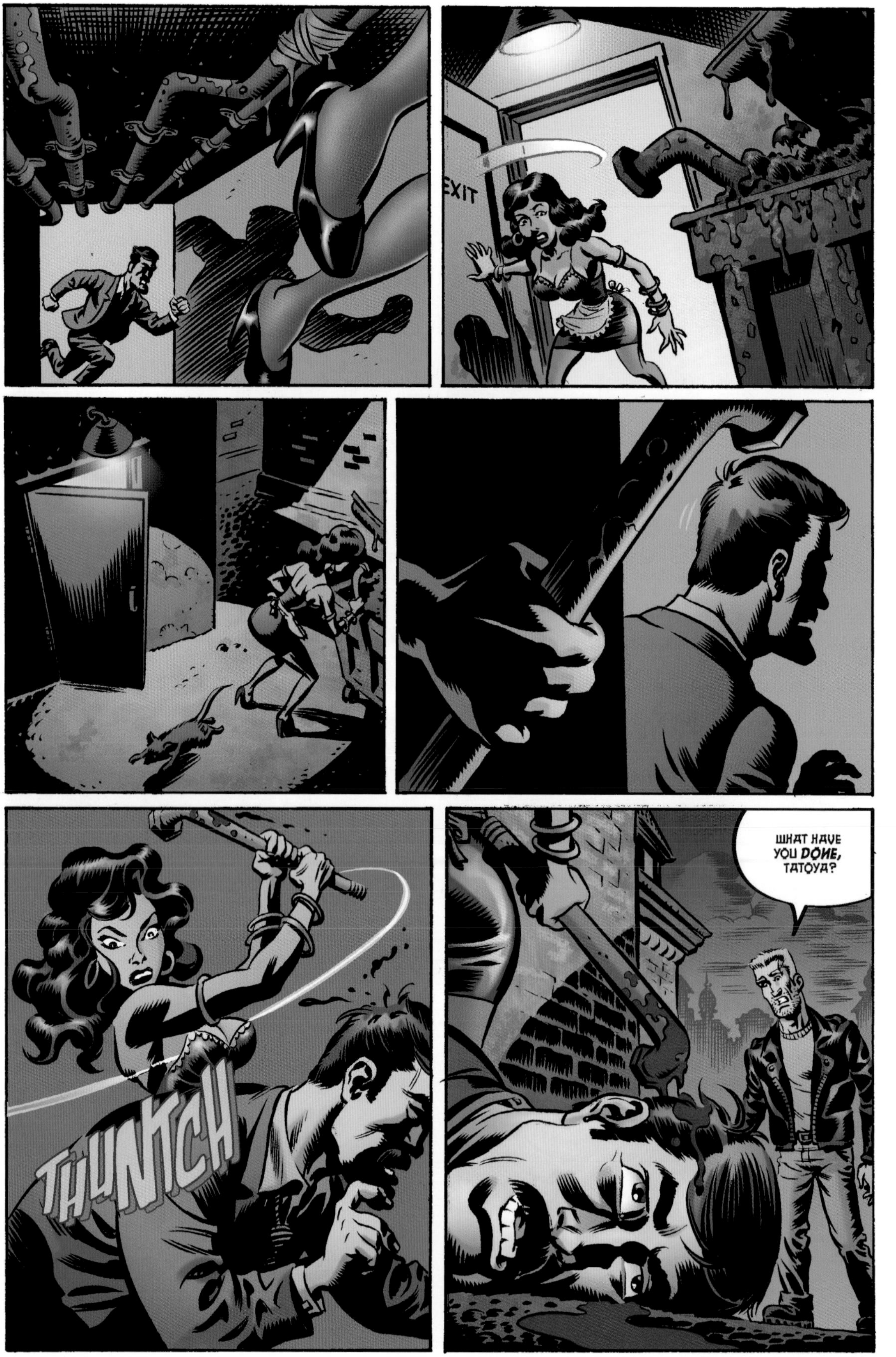
EXIT
THUNTCH
WHAT HAVE YOU DONE, TATOYA?

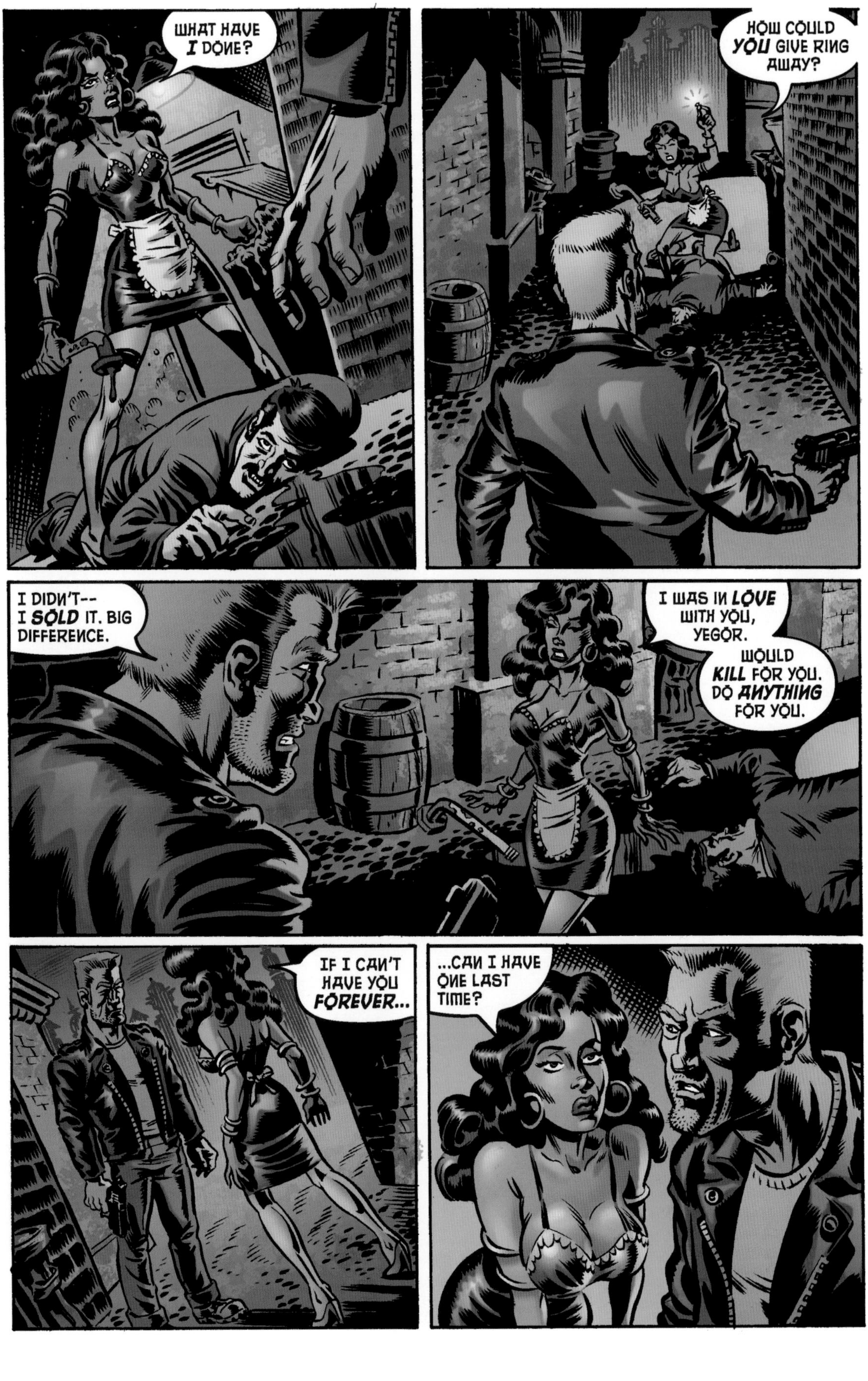
WHAT HAVE I DONE?
HOW COULD YOU GIVE RING AWAY?
I DIDN'T-- I SOLD IT. BIG DIFFERENCE.
I WAS IN LOVE WITH YOU, YEGOR.
WOULD KILL FOR YOU. DO ANYTHING FOR YOU.
IF I CAN'T HAVE YOU FOREVER...
...CAN I HAVE ONE LAST TIME?

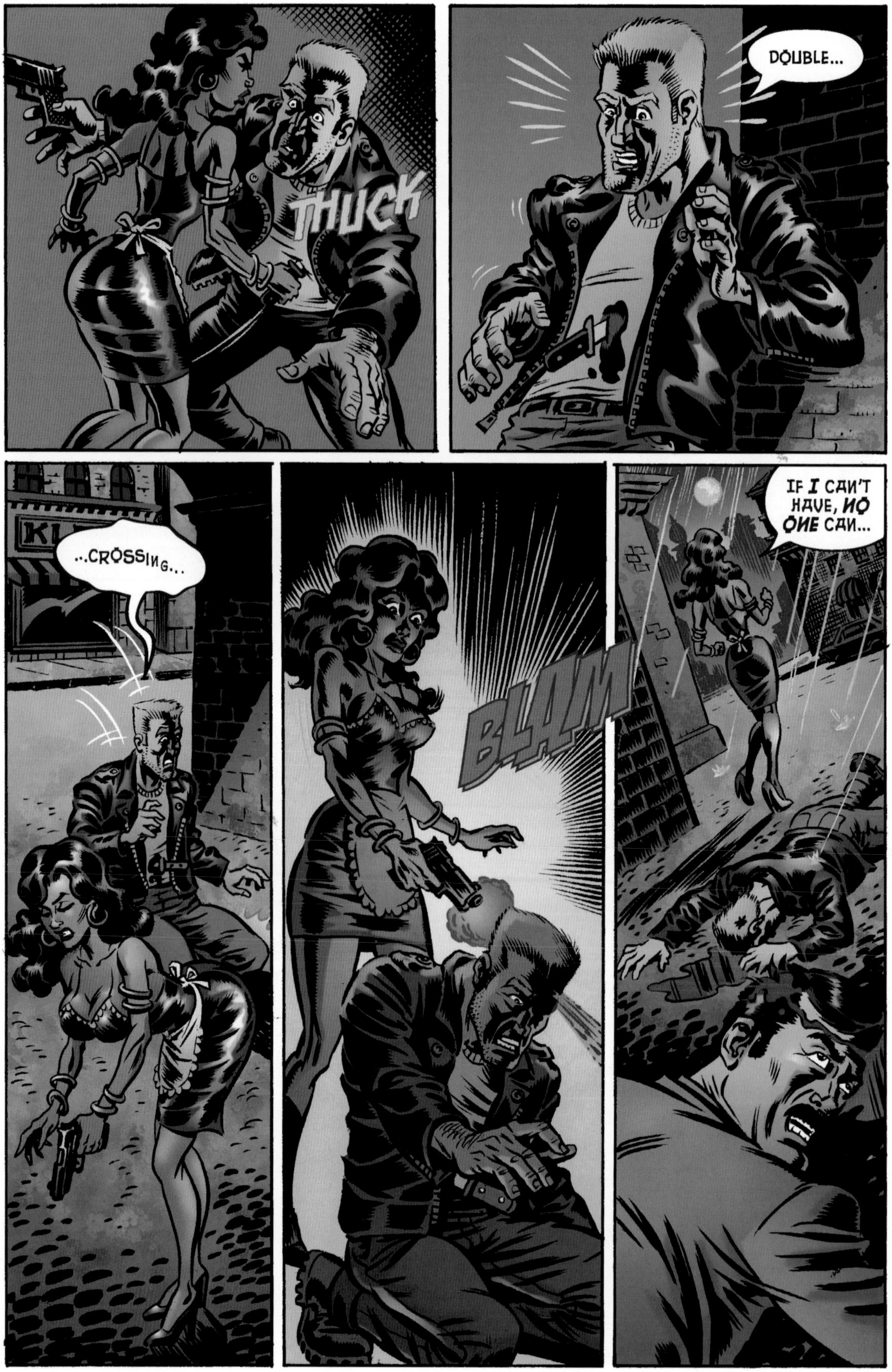
THUCK
DOUBLE...
...CROSSING...
BLAM
IF I CAN'T HAVE, NO ONE CAN...

KZZCH ...AND IN OTHER NEWS, THINGS ARE BAD ALL OVER... KZZZT

DOCTOR!

DOCTOR IVANOV!

SAY AMERICAN WILLIAM COLE IS **VEGGIE**. ALSO, OTHER MAN IS TOAST. IS **SUCKING** NEWS, DOCTOR.

ON **CONTRARY**, IS MOST **FORTUITOUS**.

BUT HAVE YET TO PITCH YOUR **DISCOVERY** TO HIM!

CALM YOURSELF, PAVEL. NO MORE **RED BEARS** FOR YOU.

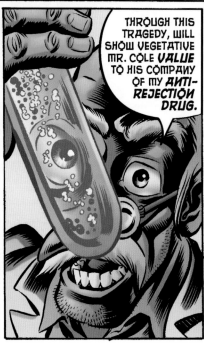

THROUGH THIS TRAGEDY, WILL SHOW VEGETATIVE MR. COLE **VALUE** TO HIS COMPANY OF MY **ANTI-REJECTION DRUG.**

BRING BODIES TO ME. **NOW!**

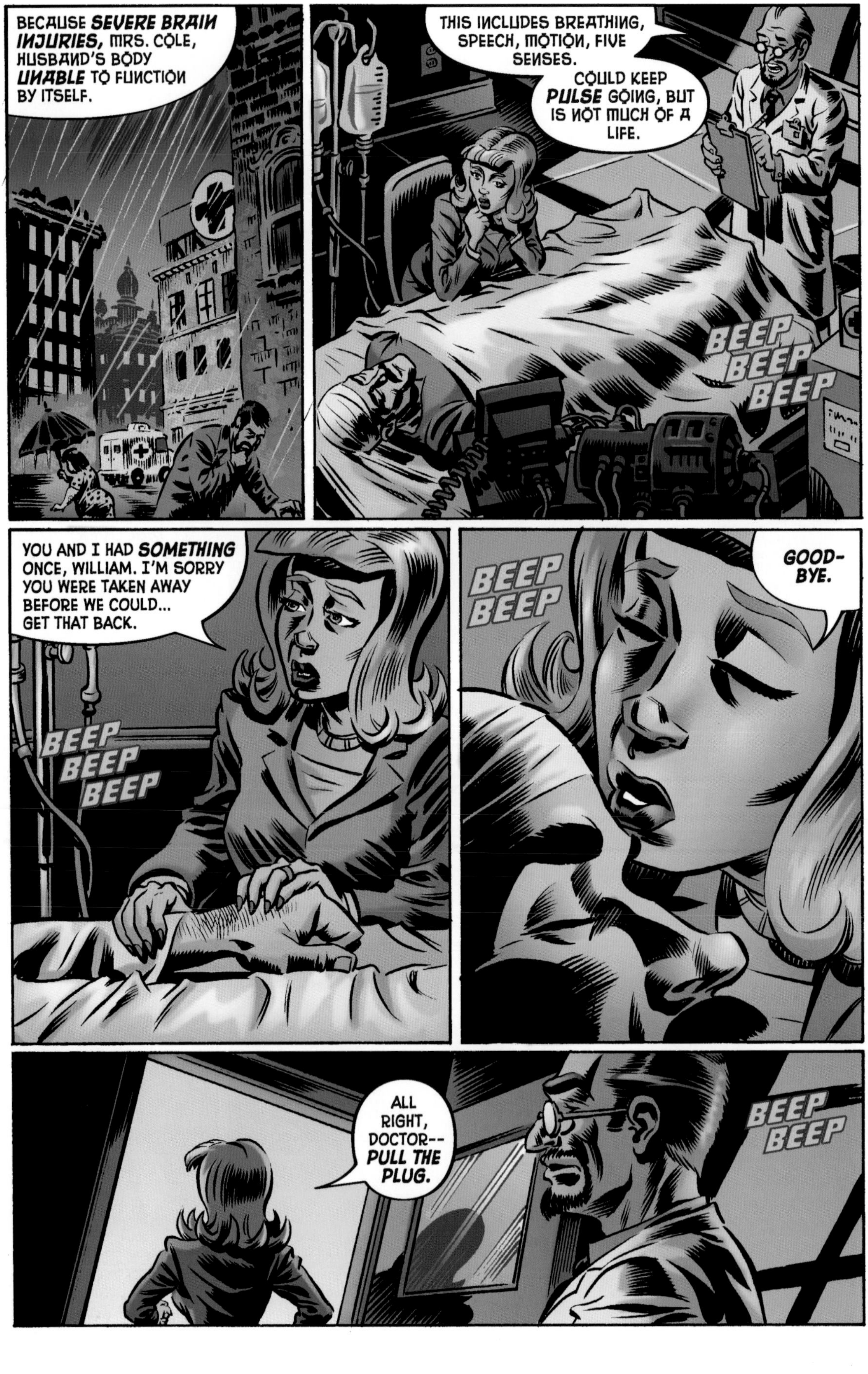

BECAUSE SEVERE BRAIN INJURIES, MRS. COLE, HUSBAND'S BODY UNABLE TO FUNCTION BY ITSELF.
THIS INCLUDES BREATHING, SPEECH, MOTION, FIVE SENSES.
COULD KEEP PULSE GOING, BUT IS NOT MUCH OF A LIFE.
BEEP BEEP BEEP
YOU AND I HAD SOMETHING ONCE, WILLIAM. I'M SORRY YOU WERE TAKEN AWAY BEFORE WE COULD... GET THAT BACK.
BEEP BEEP BEEP
BEEP BEEP
GOOD-BYE.
ALL RIGHT, DOCTOR-- PULL THE PLUG.
BEEP BEEP

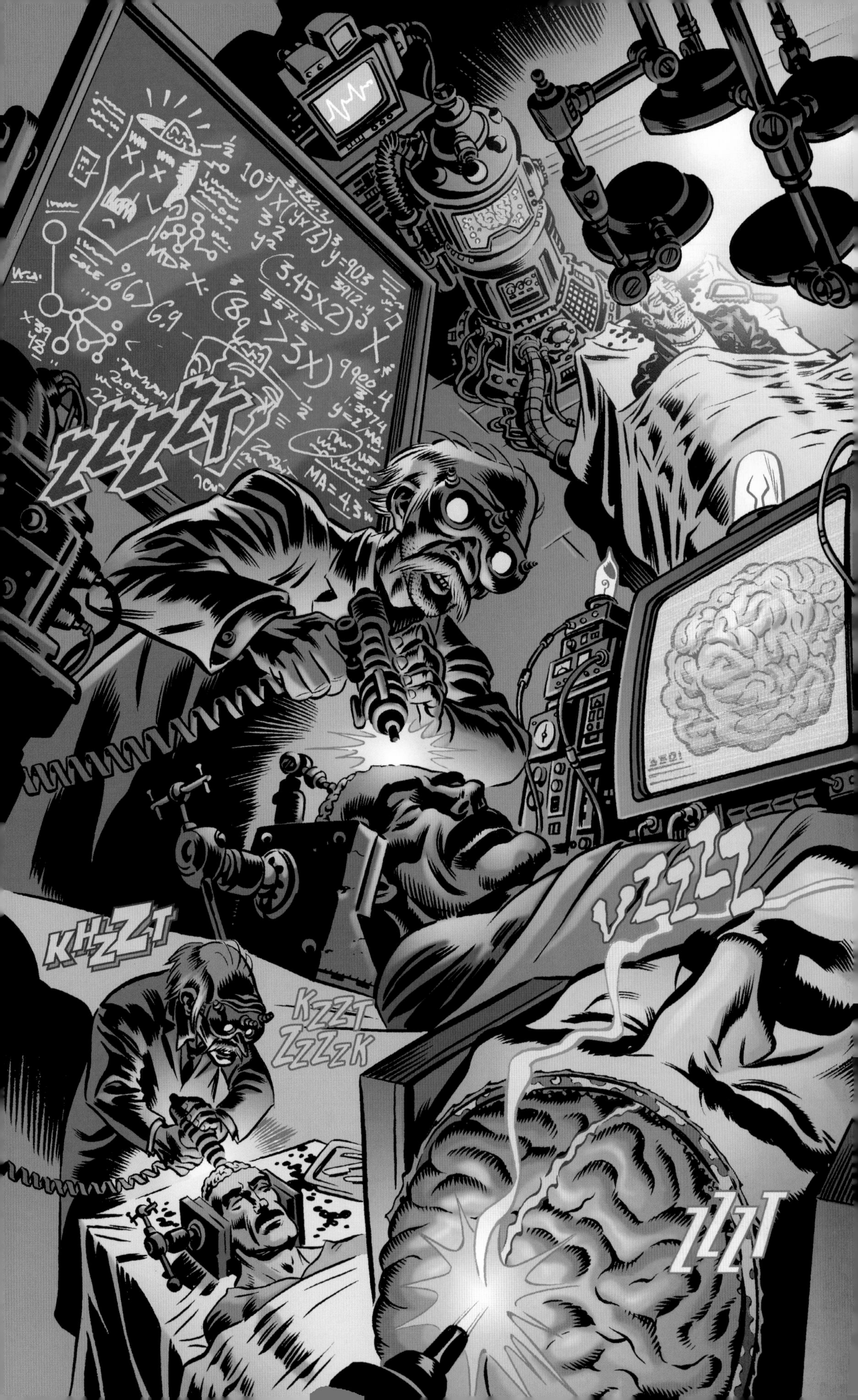
ZZZZT
VZZZZ
KHZZT
KZZT
ZZZZK
ZZZT

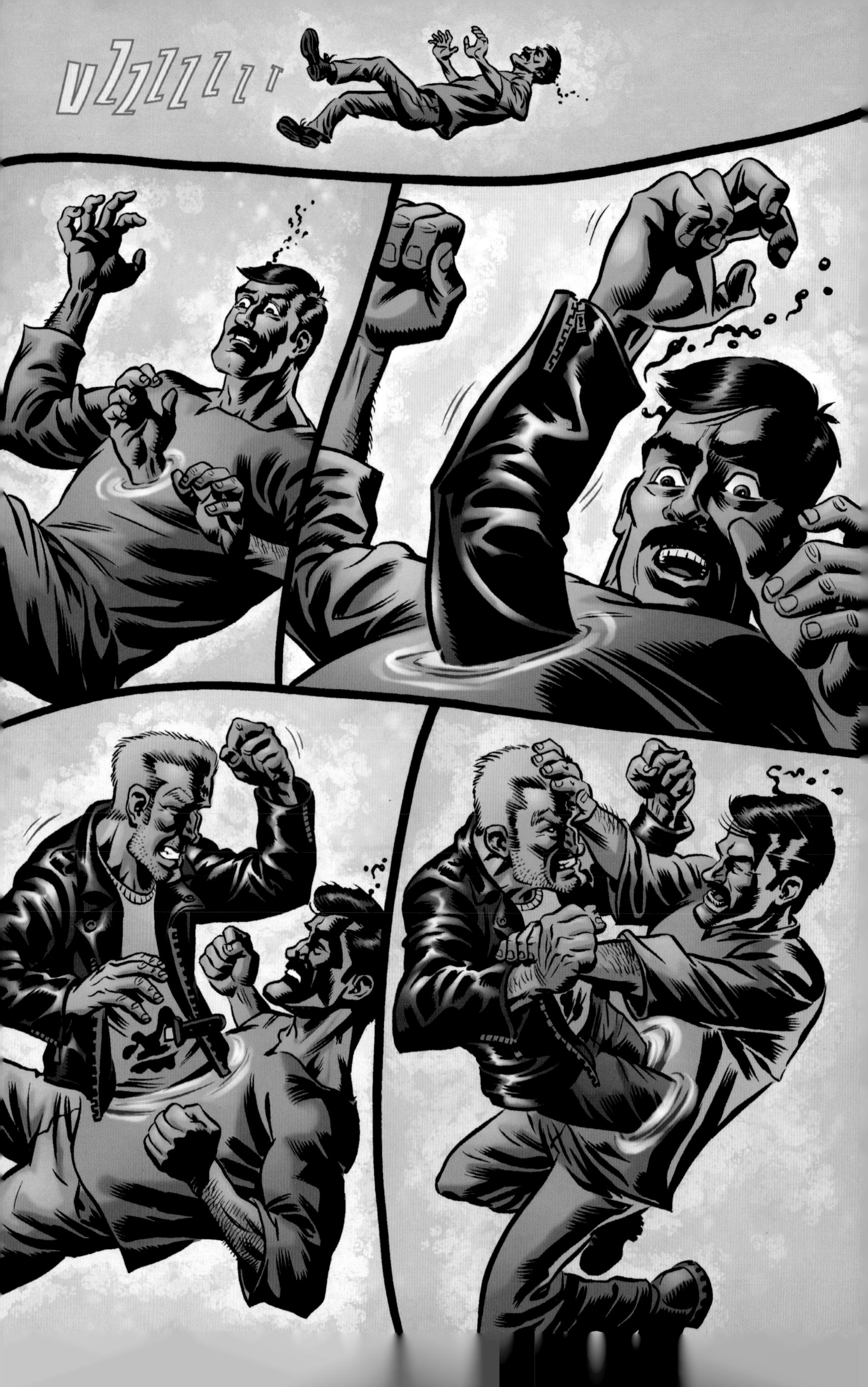
VZZZZZZZT

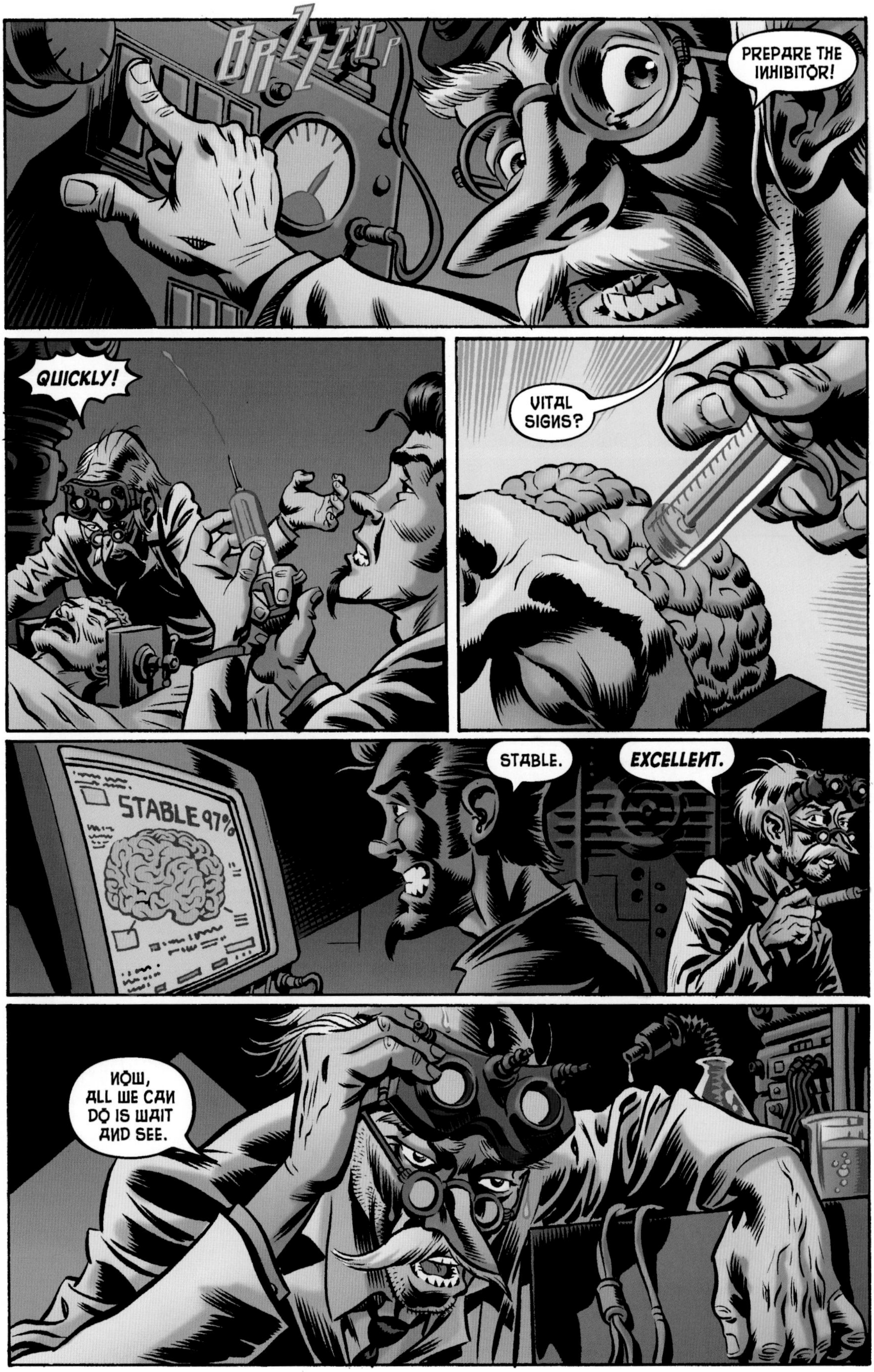
BRZZZOP
PREPARE THE INHIBITOR!
QUICKLY!
VITAL SIGNS?
STABLE 97%
STABLE.
EXCELLENT.
NOW, ALL WE CAN DO IS WAIT AND SEE.

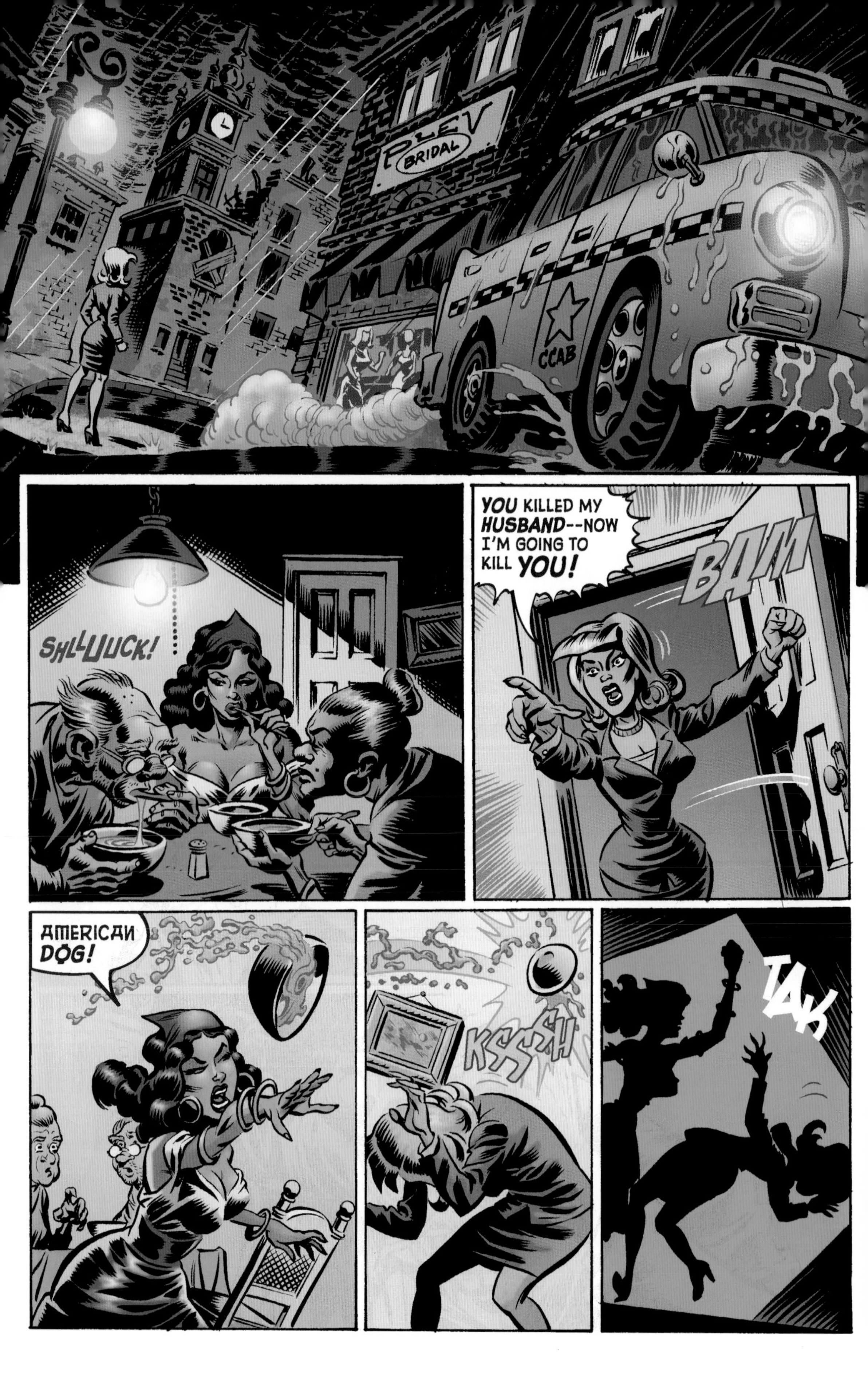
PLEV
BRIDAL
CCAB
SHLLUUCK!
YOU KILLED MY HUSBAND--NOW I'M GOING TO KILL YOU!
BAM
AMERICAN DOG!
KSSH
TAK

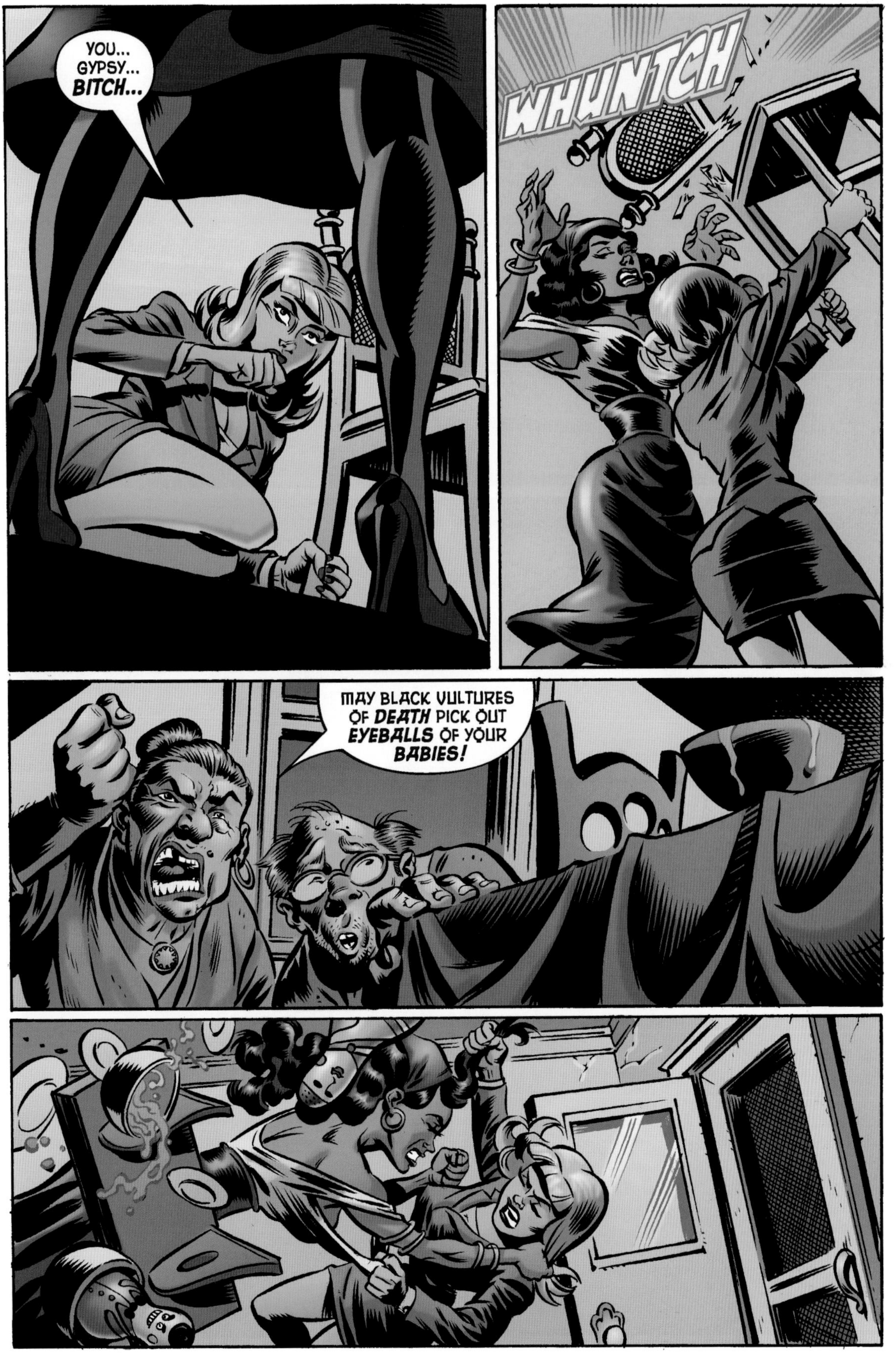
YOU... GYPSY... BITCH...
WHUNTCH
MAY BLACK VULTURES OF DEATH PICK OUT EYEBALLS OF YOUR BABIES!

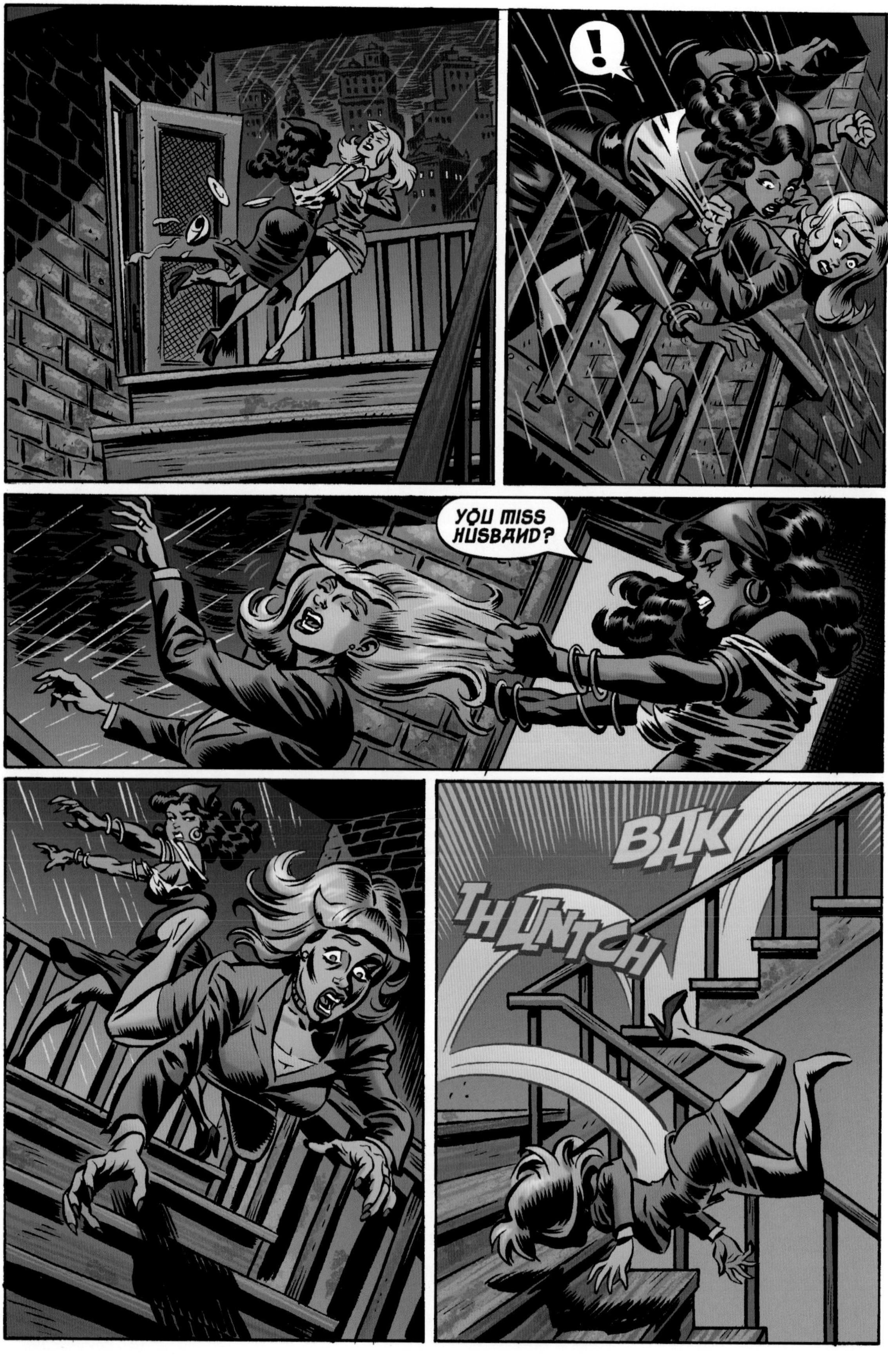
!
YOU MISS
HUSBAND?
BAK
THUNTCH

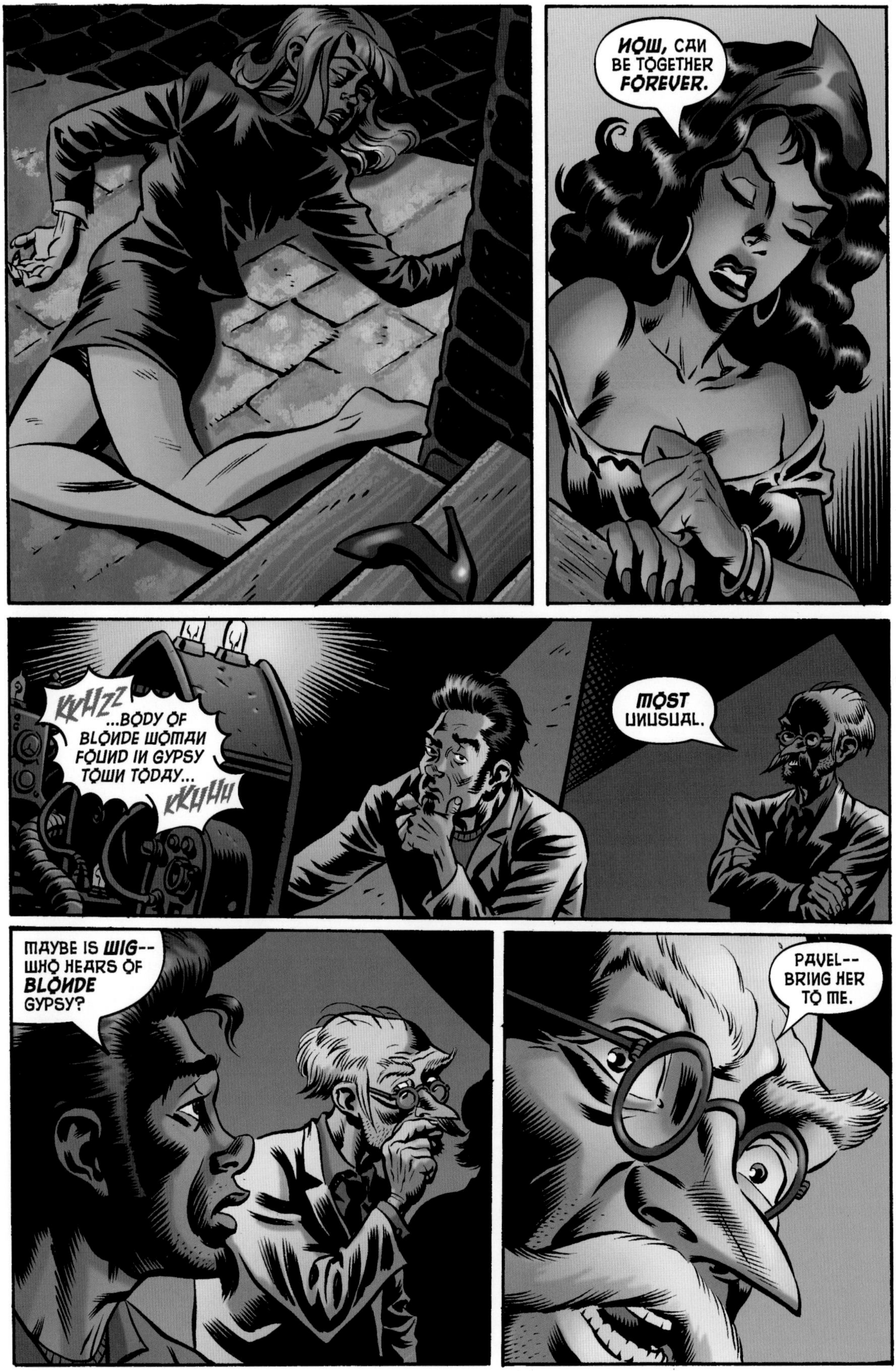
NOW, CAN BE TOGETHER FOREVER.
KKHZZ ...BODY OF BLONDE WOMAN FOUND IN GYPSY TOWN TODAY... KKHHH
MOST UNUSUAL.
MAYBE IS WIG-- WHO HEARS OF BLONDE GYPSY?
PAVEL-- BRING HER TO ME.

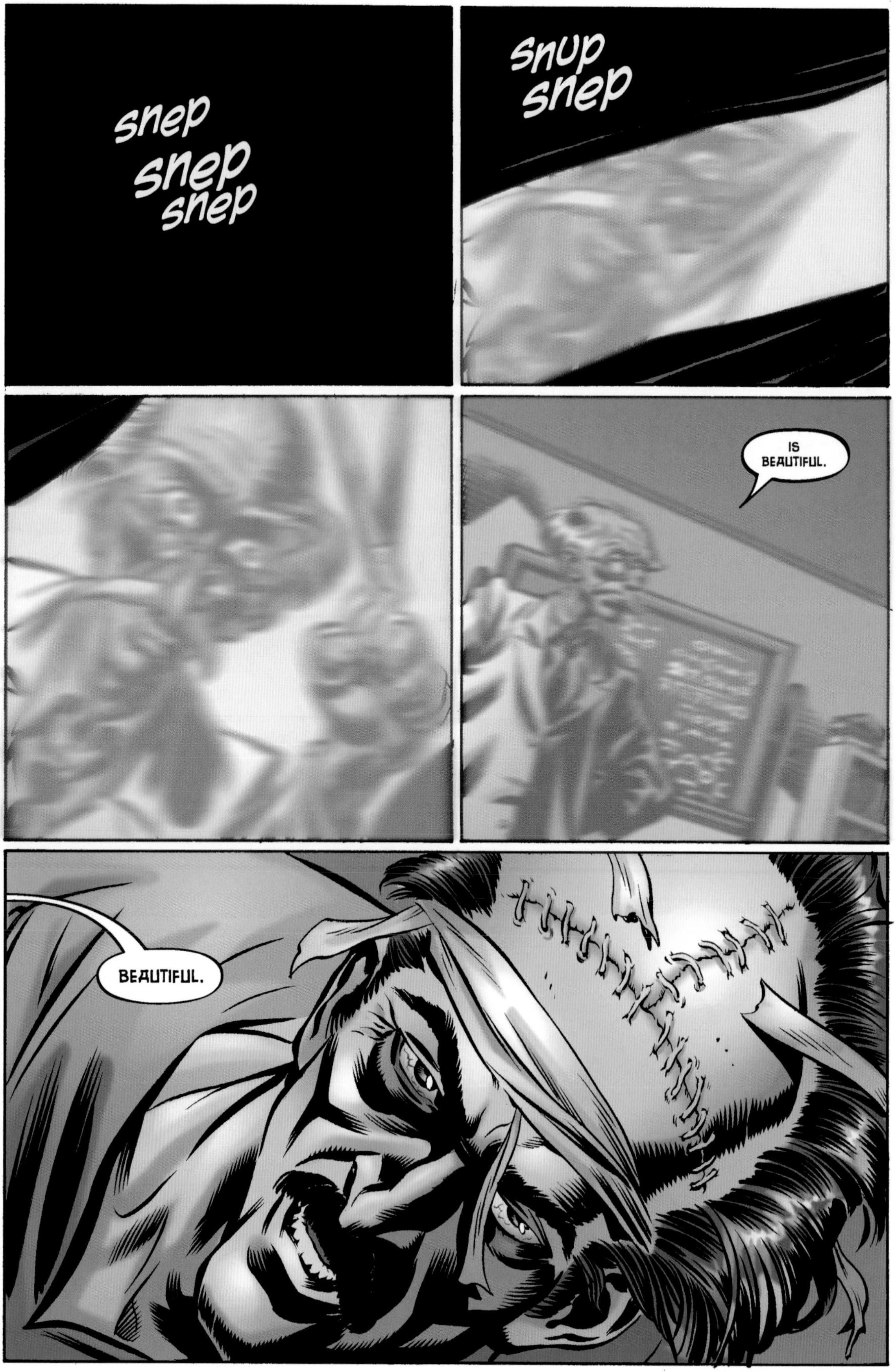
snep
snep
snep
snup
snep
IS BEAUTIFUL.
BEAUTIFUL.

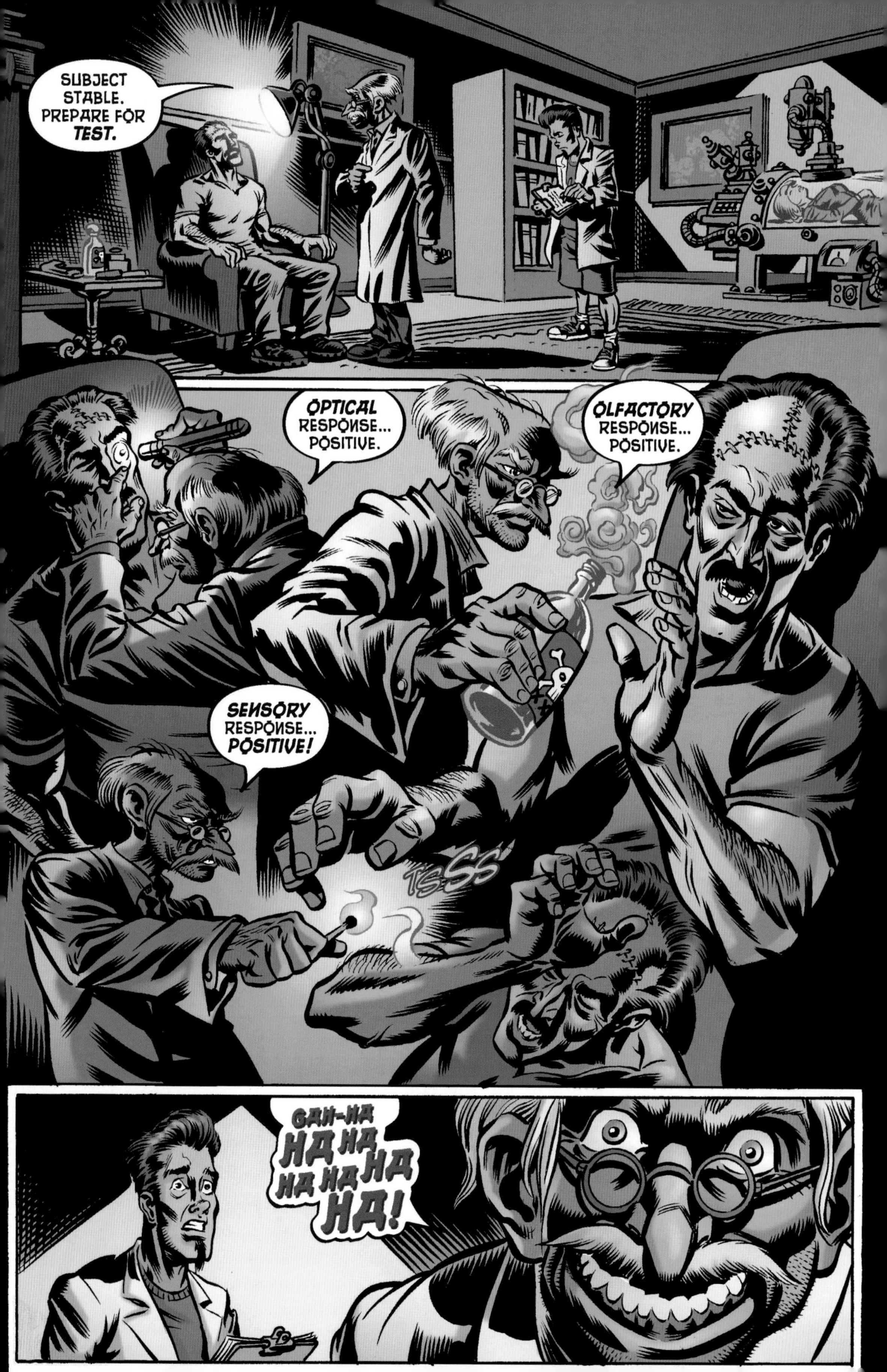
SUBJECT STABLE. PREPARE FOR TEST.
OPTICAL RESPONSE... POSITIVE.
OLFACTORY RESPONSE... POSITIVE.
SENSORY RESPONSE... POSITIVE!
TSSSS
GAH-HA HA HA HA HA HA HA!

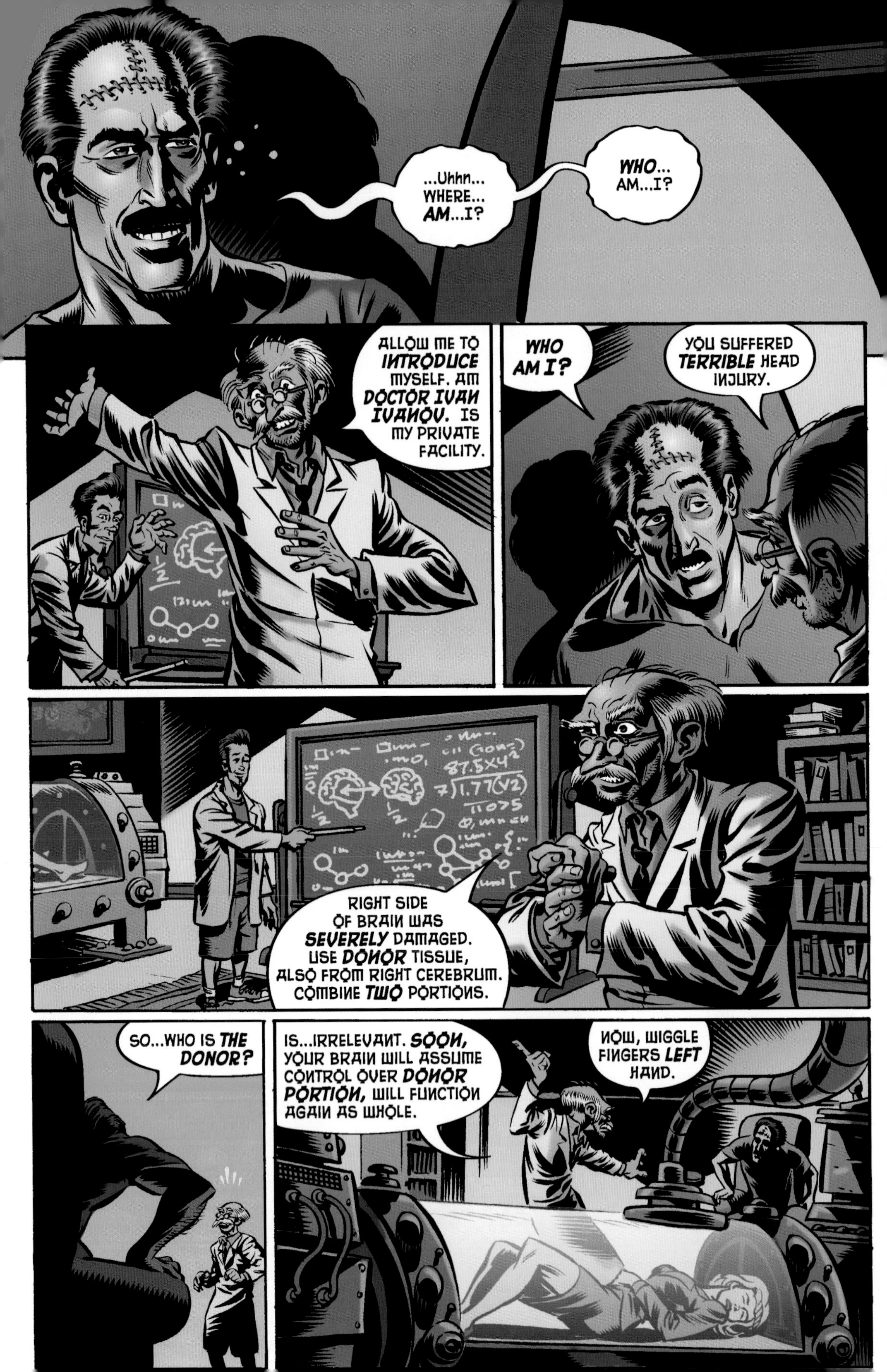
...Uhhn... WHERE... AM...I?
WHO... AM...I?
ALLOW ME TO INTRODUCE MYSELF. AM DOCTOR IVAN IVANOV. IS MY PRIVATE FACILITY.
WHO AM I?
YOU SUFFERED TERRIBLE HEAD INJURY.
RIGHT SIDE OF BRAIN WAS SEVERELY DAMAGED. USE DONOR TISSUE, ALSO FROM RIGHT CEREBRUM. COMBINE TWO PORTIONS.
SO...WHO IS THE DONOR?
IS...IRRELEVANT. SOON, YOUR BRAIN WILL ASSUME CONTROL OVER DONOR PORTION, WILL FUNCTION AGAIN AS WHOLE.
NOW, WIGGLE FINGERS LEFT HAND.

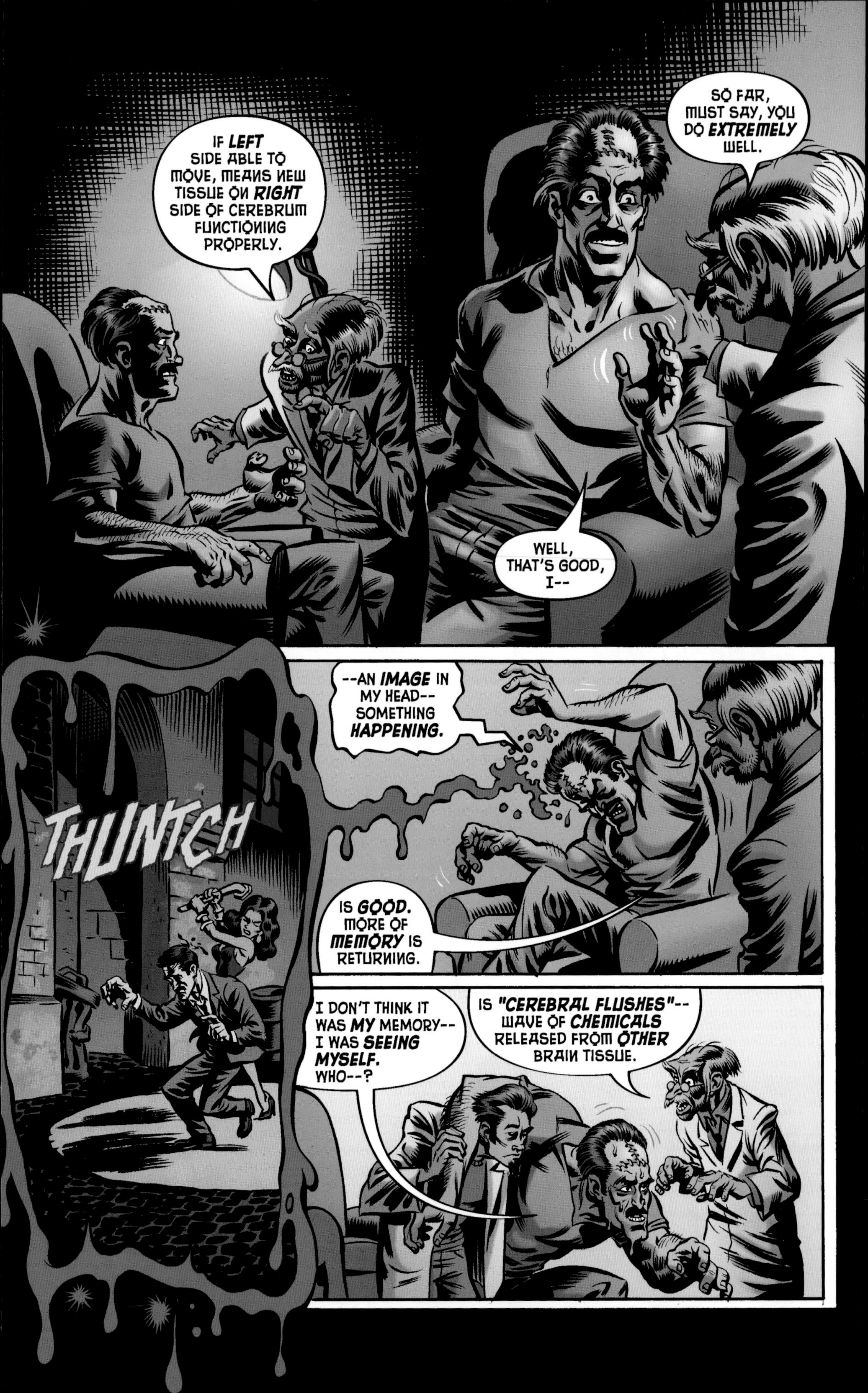
IF LEFT SIDE ABLE TO MOVE, MEANS NEW TISSUE ON RIGHT SIDE OF CEREBRUM FUNCTIONING PROPERLY.
SO FAR, MUST SAY, YOU DO EXTREMELY WELL.
WELL, THAT'S GOOD, I--
THUNTCH
--AN IMAGE IN MY HEAD-- SOMETHING HAPPENING.
IS GOOD. MORE OF MEMORY IS RETURNING.
I DON'T THINK IT WAS MY MEMORY-- I WAS SEEING MYSELF. WHO--?
IS "CEREBRAL FLUSHES"-- WAVE OF CHEMICALS RELEASED FROM OTHER BRAIN TISSUE.

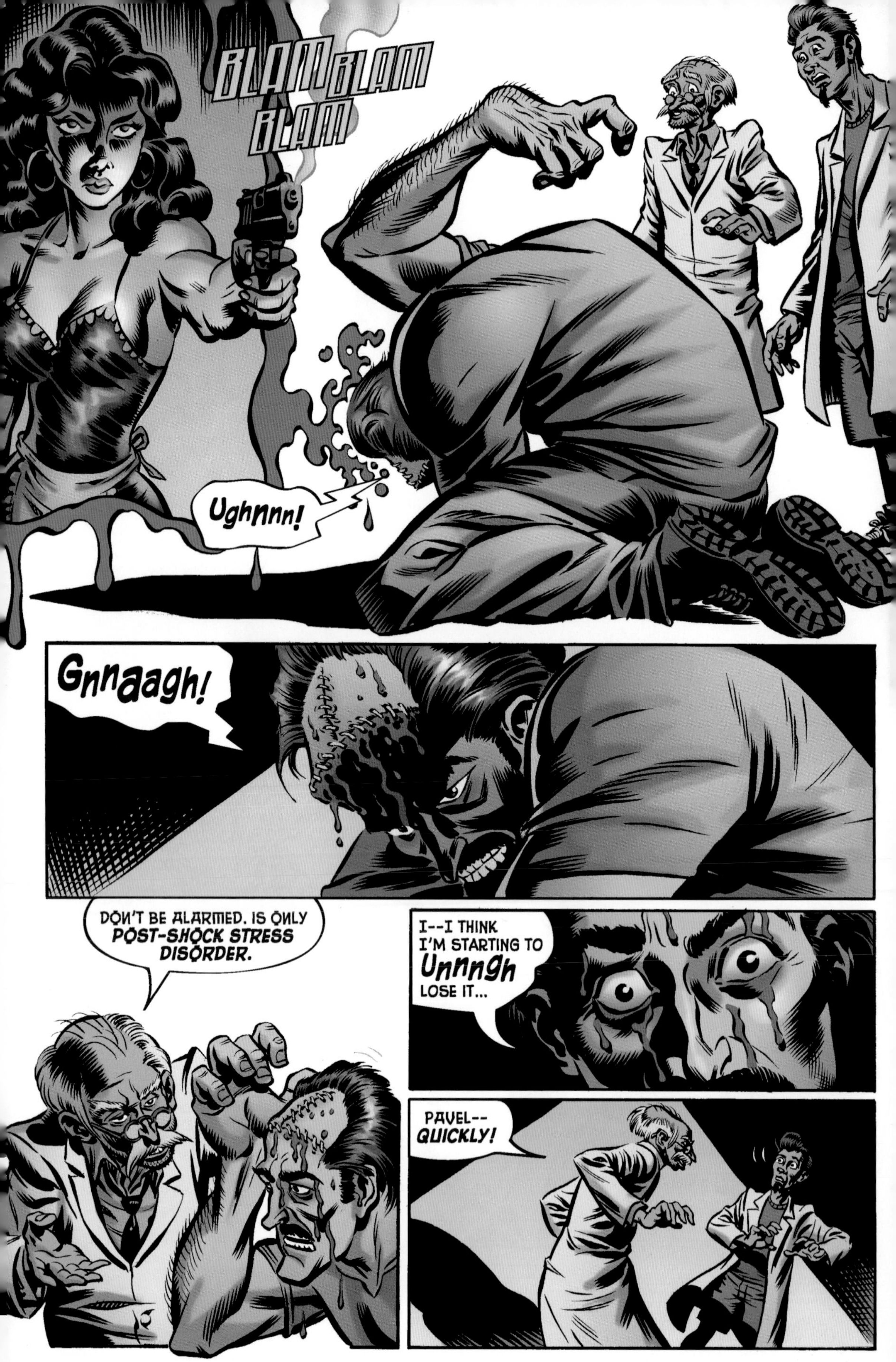
BLAM BLAM BLAM
Ughnnn!
Gnnaagh!
DON'T BE ALARMED. IS ONLY POST-SHOCK STRESS DISORDER.
I--I THINK I'M STARTING TO Unnngh LOSE IT...
PAVEL-- QUICKLY!

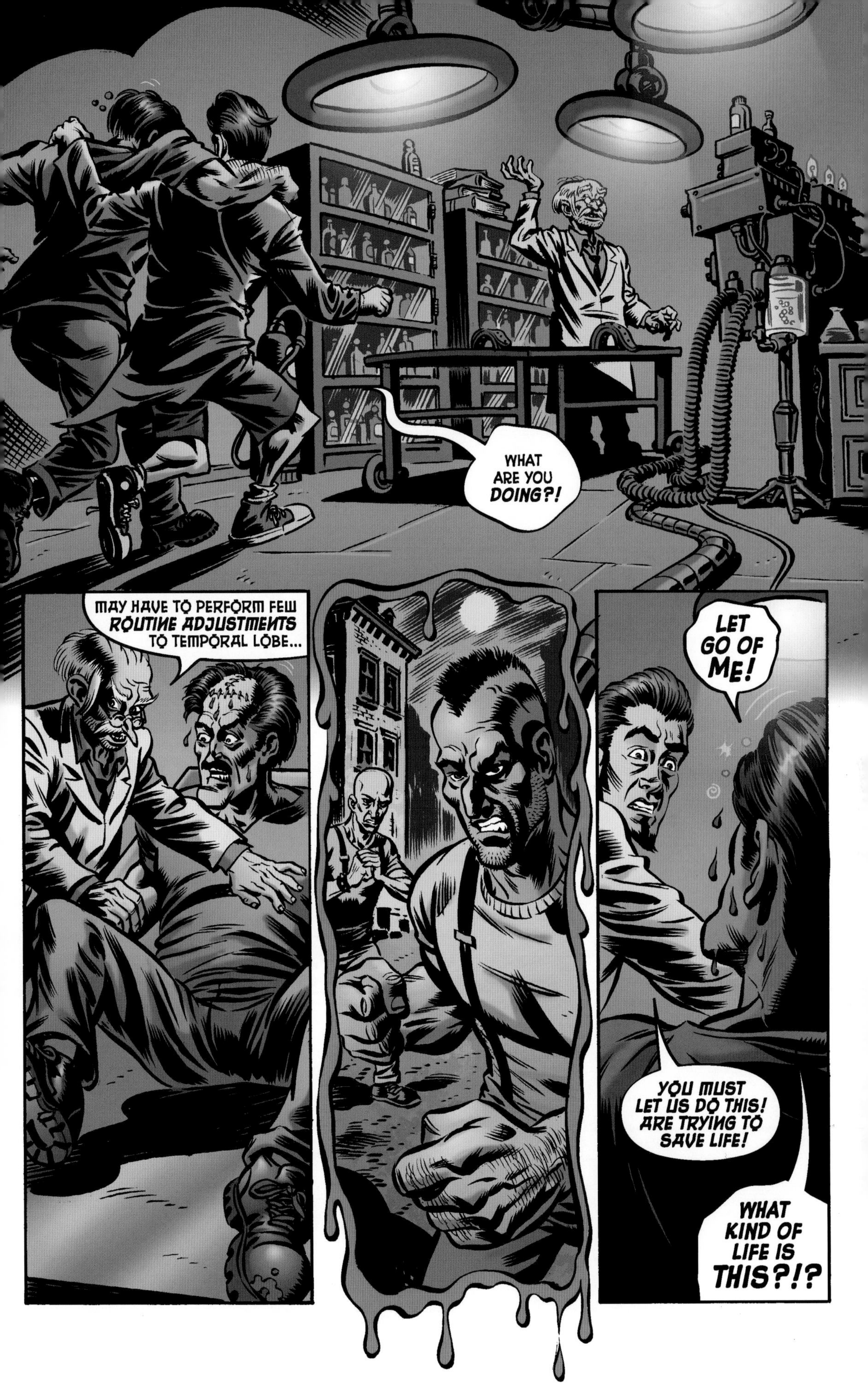
WHAT ARE YOU DOING?!
MAY HAVE TO PERFORM FEW ROUTINE ADJUSTMENTS TO TEMPORAL LOBE...
LET GO OF ME!
YOU MUST LET US DO THIS! ARE TRYING TO SAVE LIFE!
WHAT KIND OF LIFE IS THIS?!?

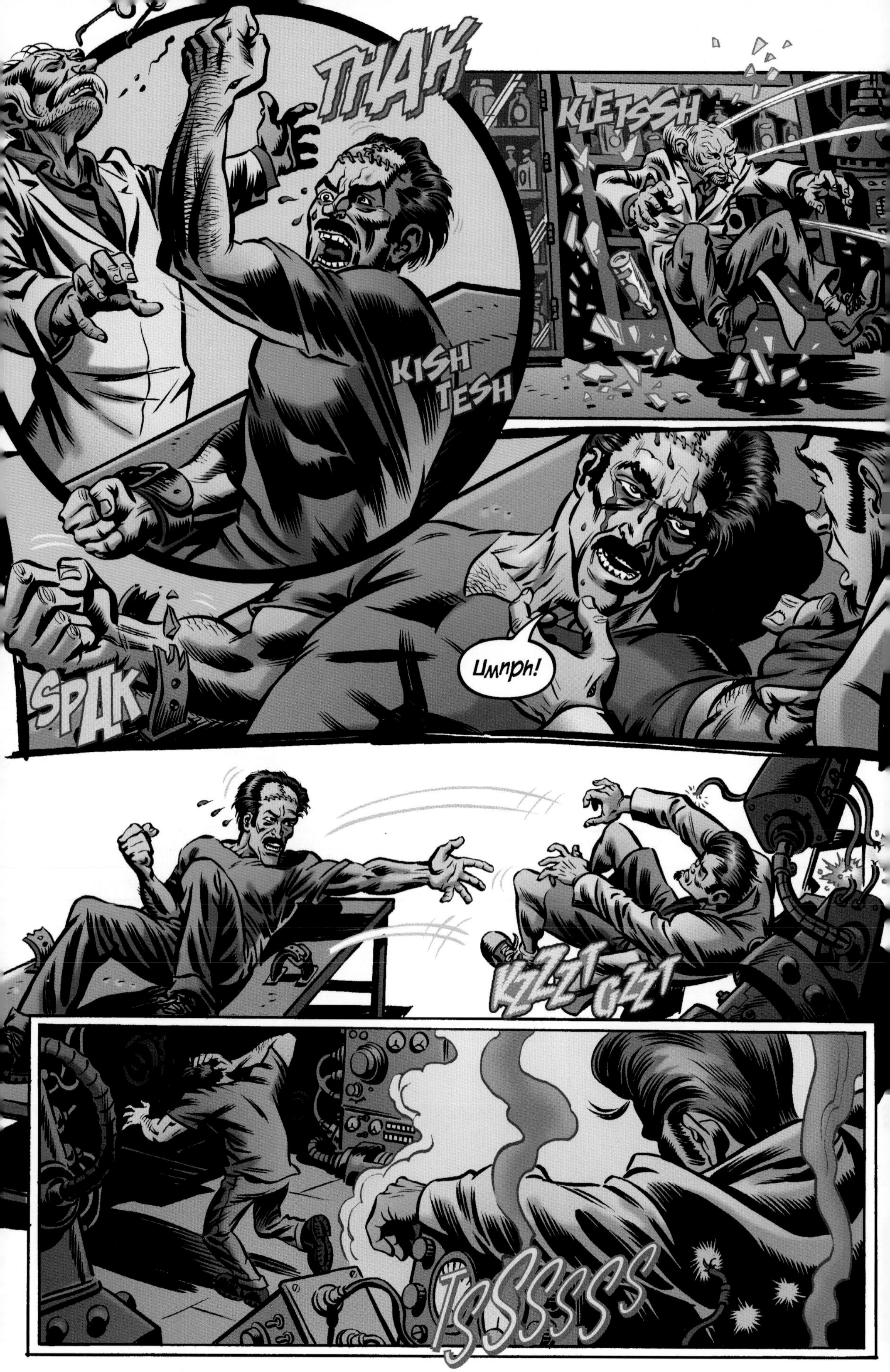
THAK
KLETSSH
KISH TESH
SPAK
Umnph!
KZZZT GZZT
TSSSSSS

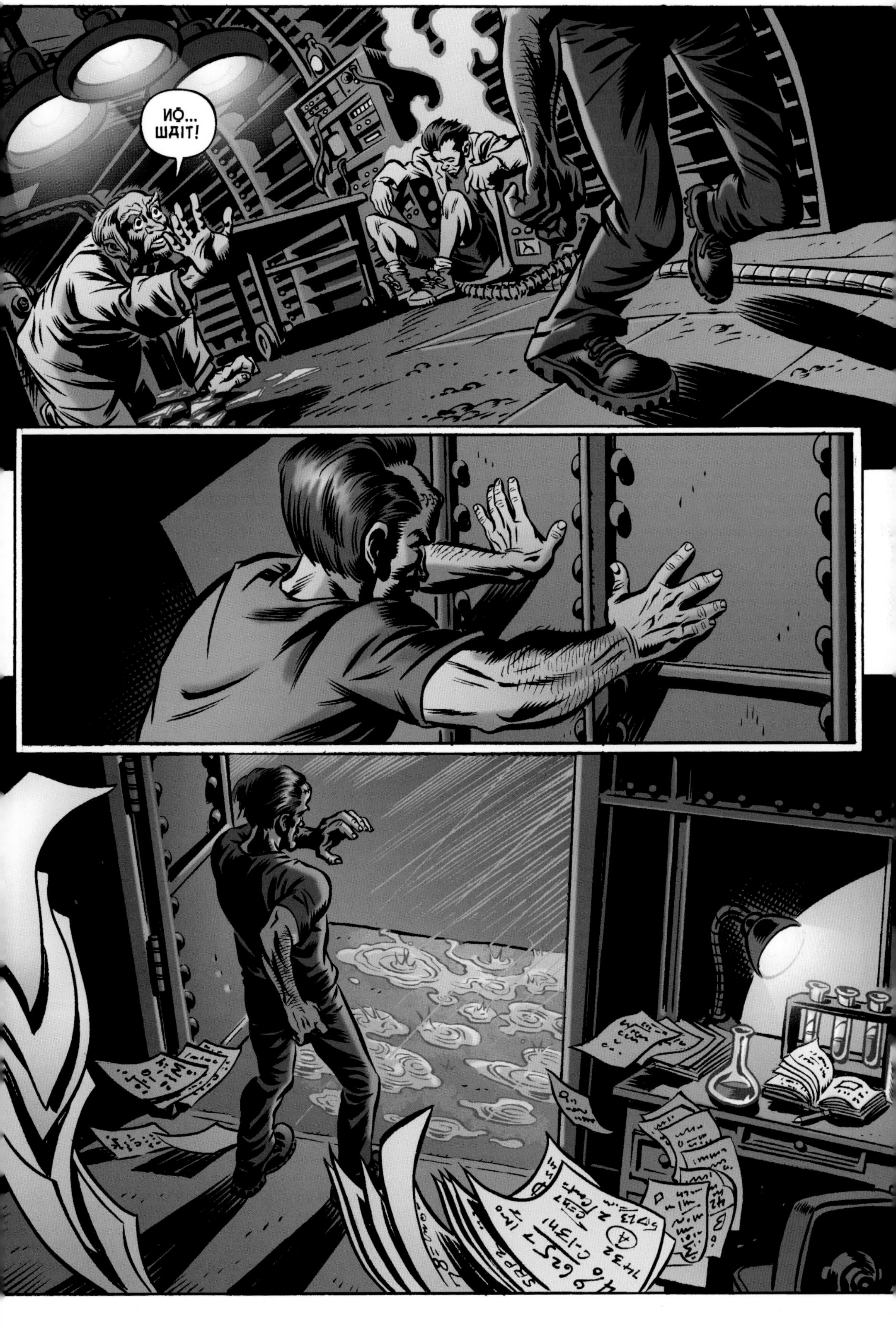
NO... WAIT!

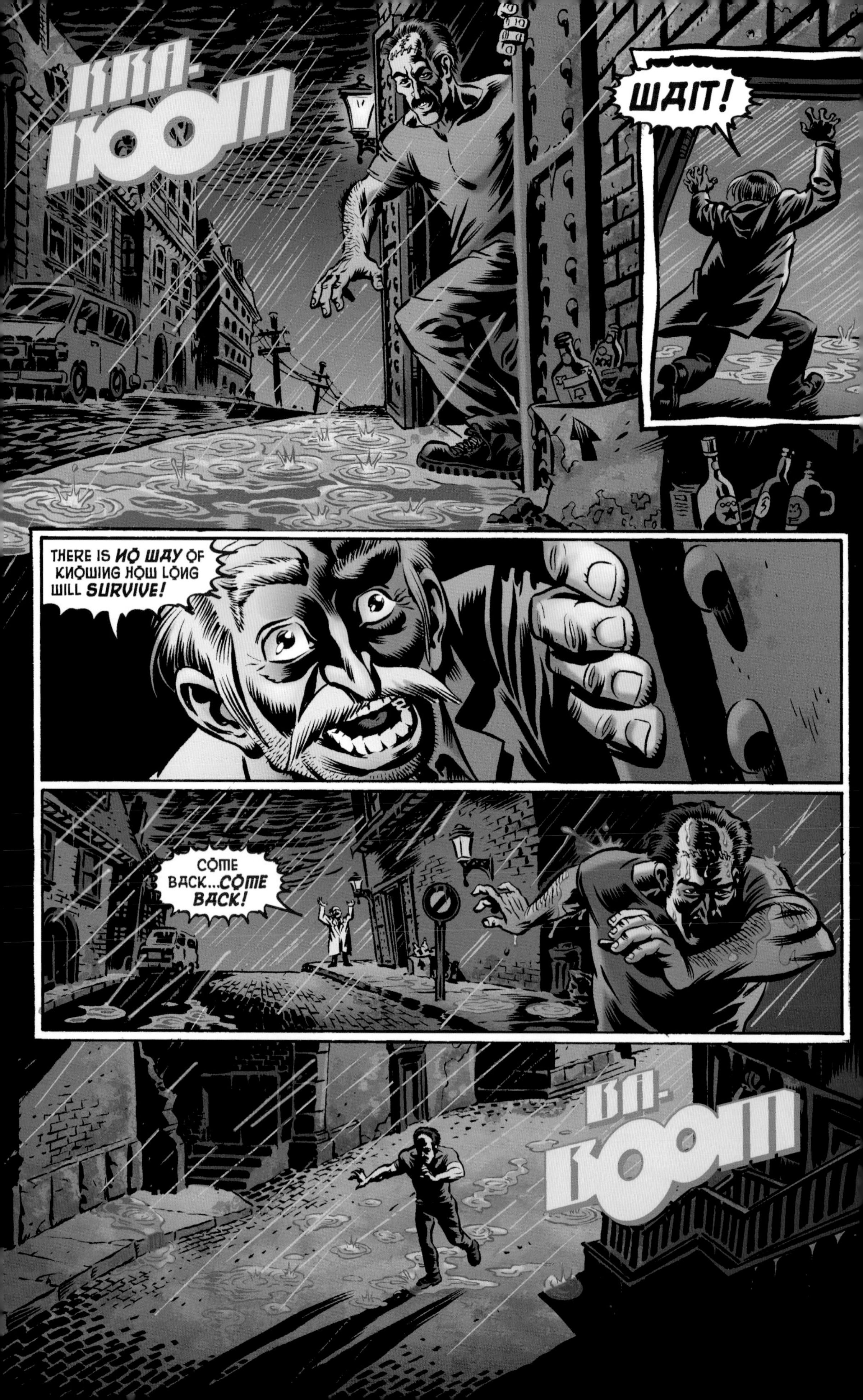
KRA-KOOM
WAIT!
THERE IS NO WAY OF KNOWING HOW LONG WILL SURVIVE!
COME BACK...COME BACK!
BA-BOOM

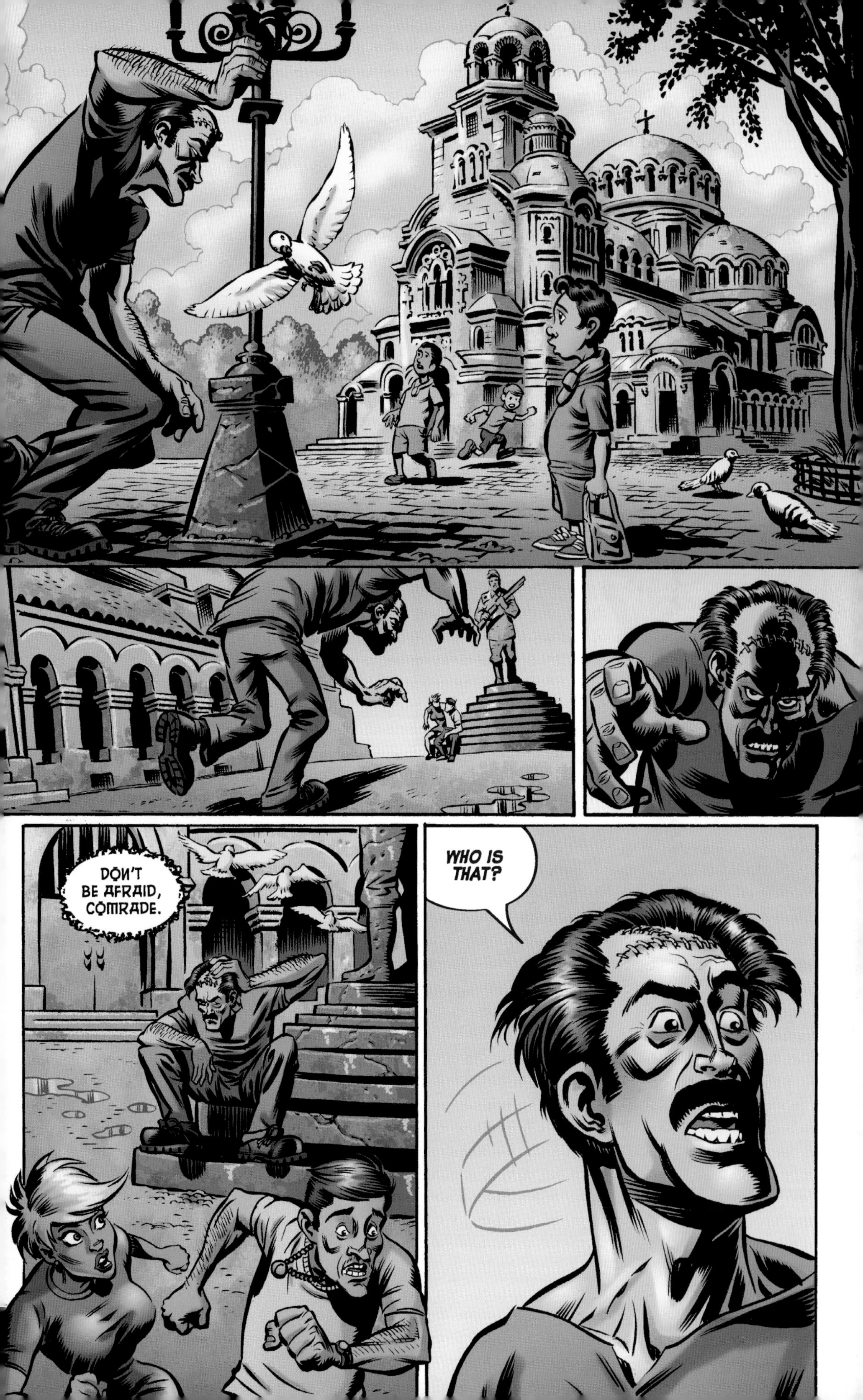
DON'T
BE AFRAID,
COMRADE.
WHO IS
THAT?

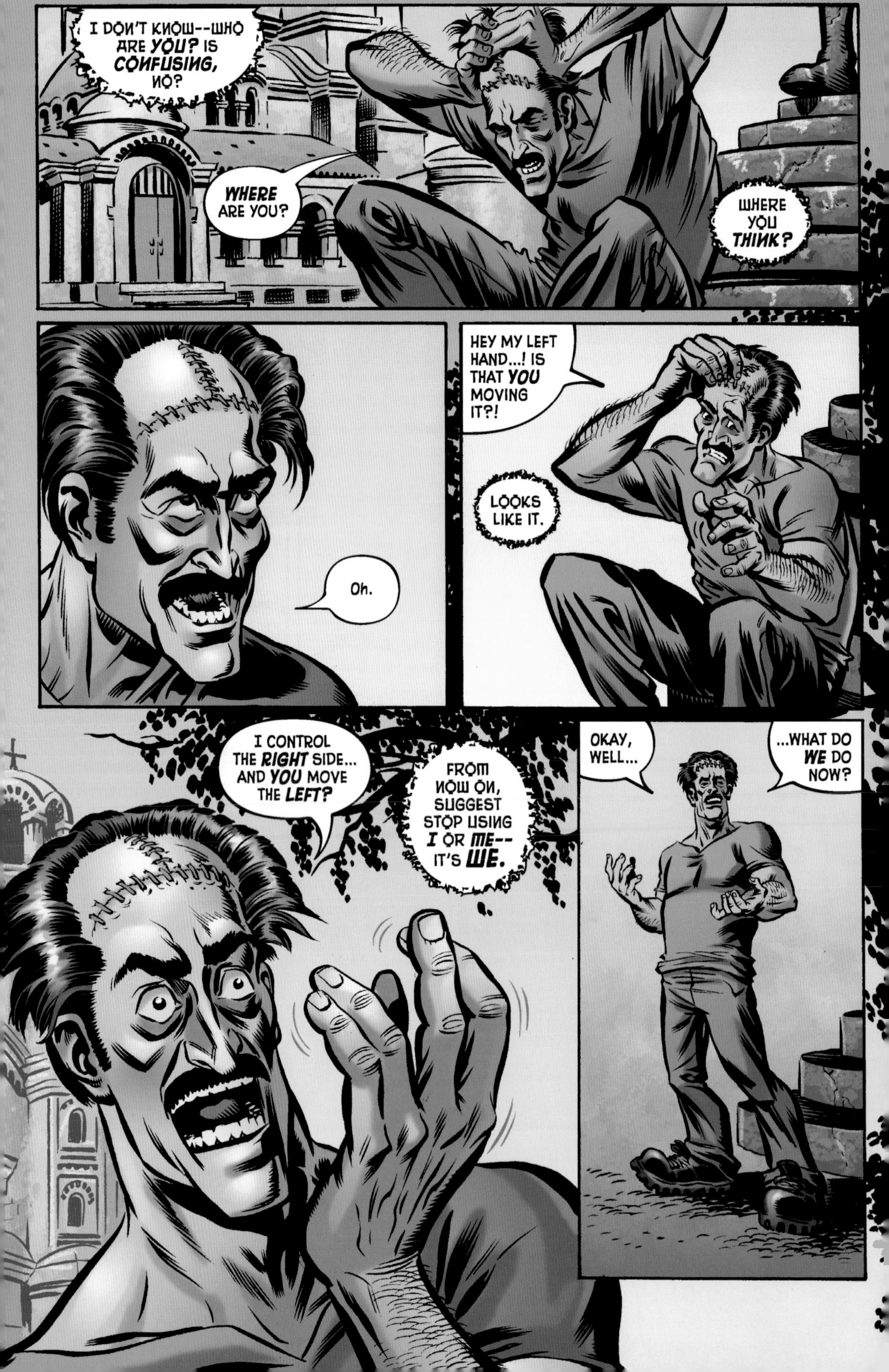
I DON'T KNOW--WHO ARE YOU? IS CONFUSING, NO?
WHERE ARE YOU?
WHERE YOU THINK?
HEY MY LEFT HAND...! IS THAT YOU MOVING IT?!
LOOKS LIKE IT.
Oh.
I CONTROL THE RIGHT SIDE... AND YOU MOVE THE LEFT?
FROM NOW ON, SUGGEST STOP USING I OR ME--IT'S WE.
OKAY, WELL...
...WHAT DO WE DO NOW?

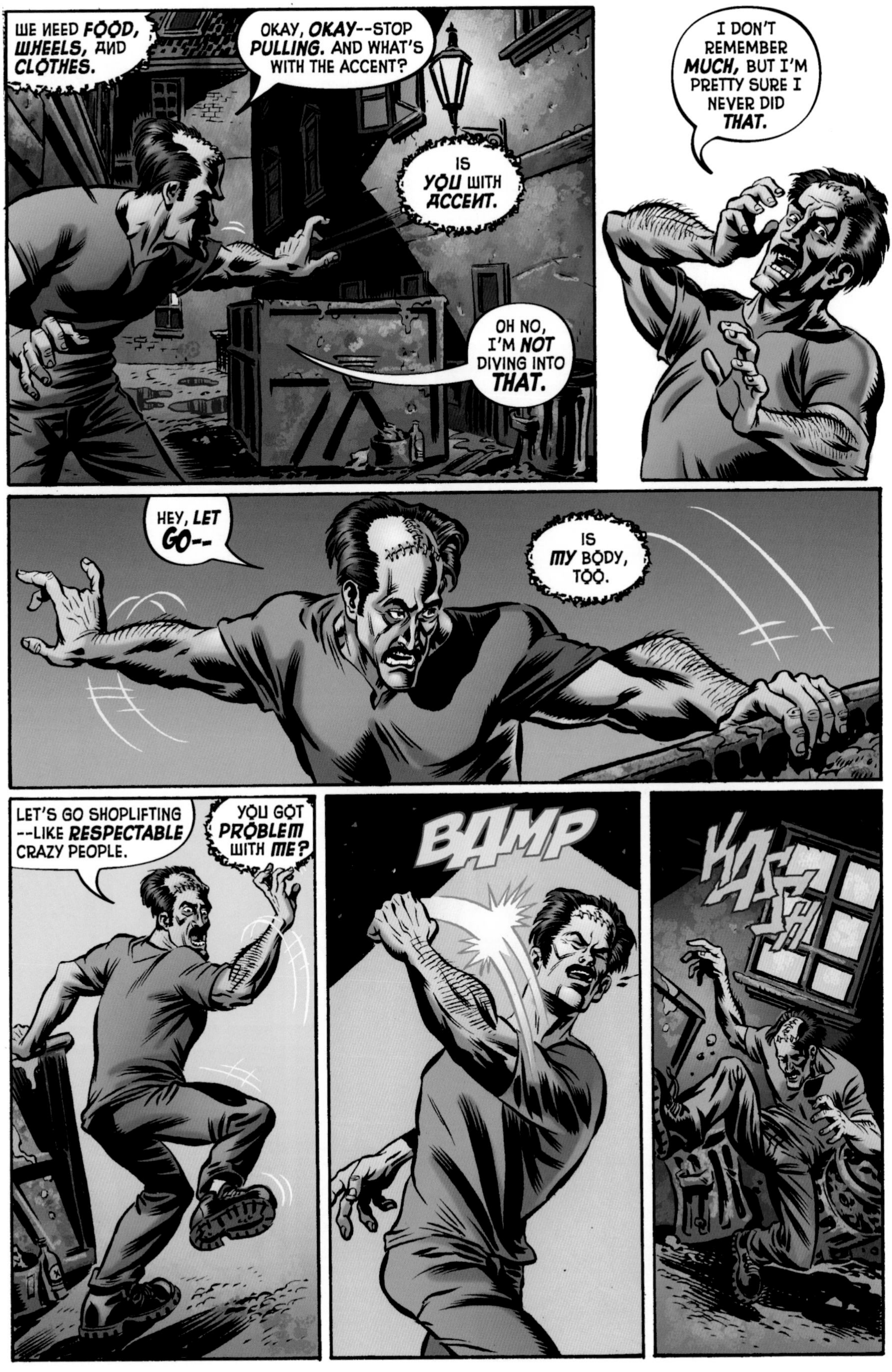
WE NEED FOOD, WHEELS, AND CLOTHES.
OKAY, OKAY--STOP PULLING. AND WHAT'S WITH THE ACCENT?
IS YOU WITH ACCENT.
OH NO, I'M NOT DIVING INTO THAT.
I DON'T REMEMBER MUCH, BUT I'M PRETTY SURE I NEVER DID THAT.
HEY, LET GO--
IS MY BODY, TOO.
LET'S GO SHOPLIFTING --LIKE RESPECTABLE CRAZY PEOPLE.
YOU GOT PROBLEM WITH ME?
BAMP
KASSH

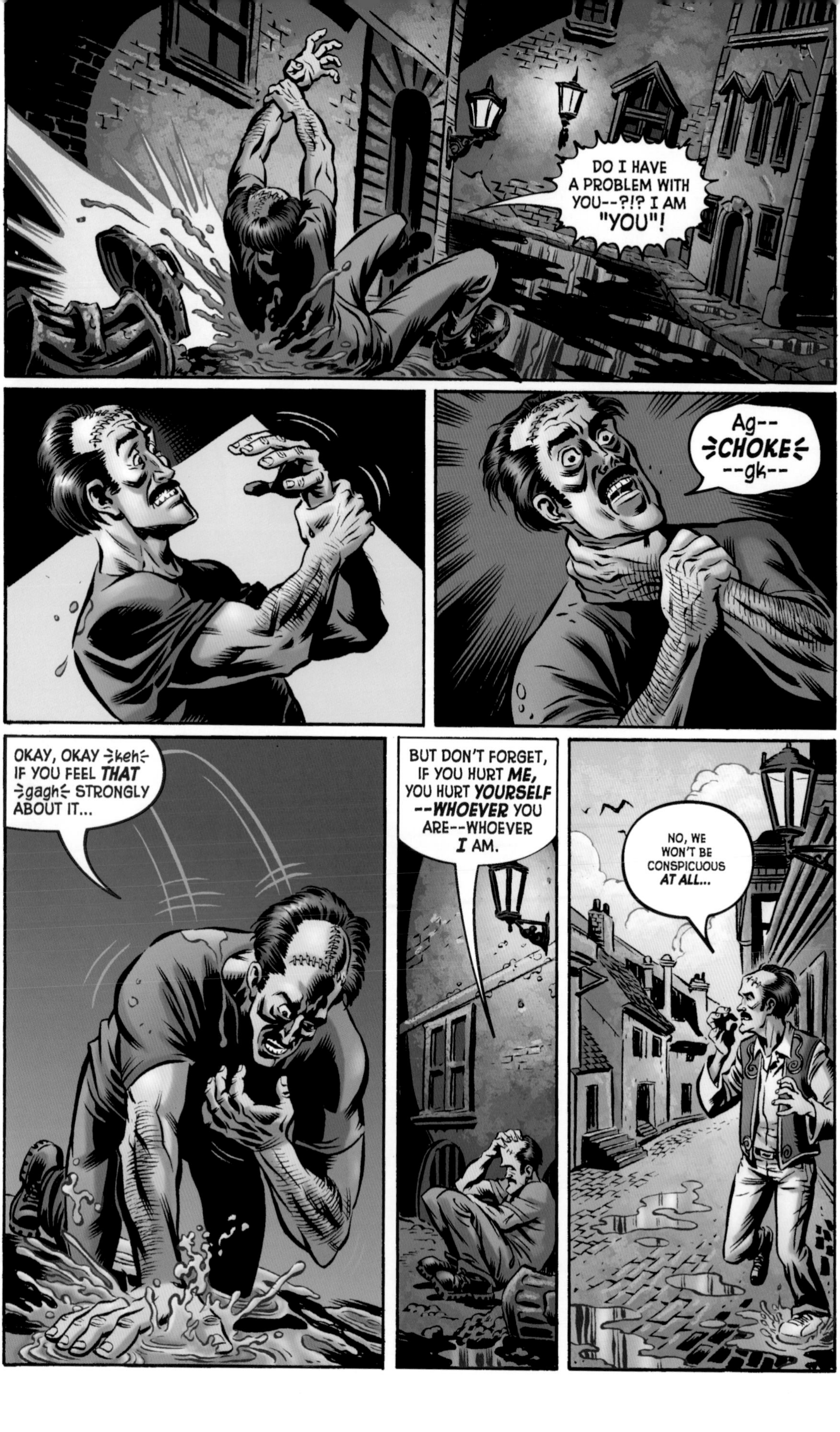
DO I HAVE A PROBLEM WITH YOU--?!? I AM "YOU"!
Ag-- CHOKE --gk--
OKAY, OKAY keh IF YOU FEEL THAT gagh STRONGLY ABOUT IT...
BUT DON'T FORGET, IF YOU HURT ME, YOU HURT YOURSELF --WHOEVER YOU ARE--WHOEVER I AM.
NO, WE WON'T BE CONSPICUOUS AT ALL...

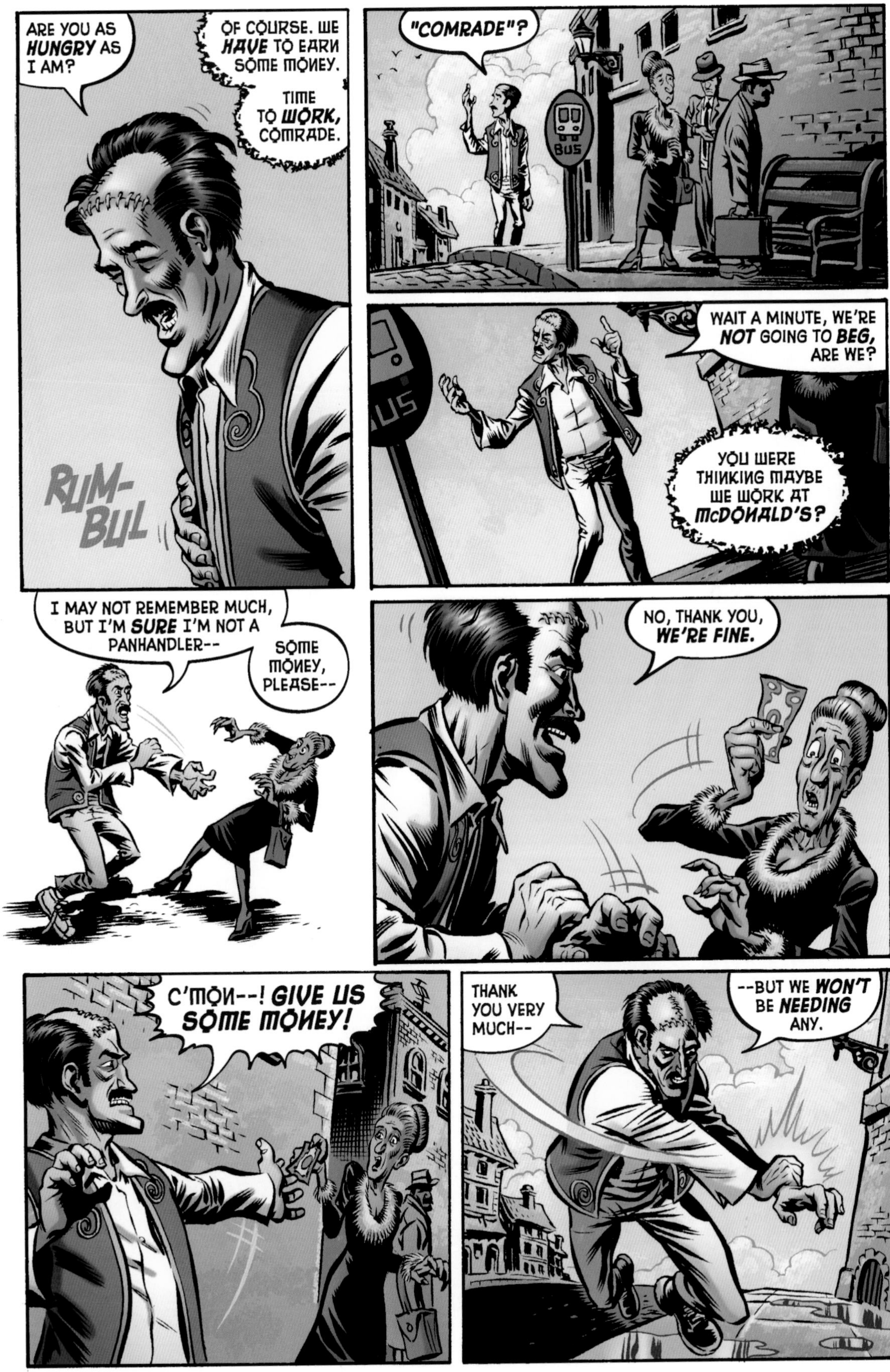
ARE YOU AS HUNGRY AS I AM?
OF COURSE. WE HAVE TO EARN SOME MONEY.
TIME TO WORK, COMRADE.
RUM-BUL
"COMRADE"?
BUS
WAIT A MINUTE, WE'RE NOT GOING TO BEG, ARE WE?
YOU WERE THINKING MAYBE WE WORK AT McDONALD'S?
I MAY NOT REMEMBER MUCH, BUT I'M SURE I'M NOT A PANHANDLER--
SOME MONEY, PLEASE--
NO, THANK YOU, WE'RE FINE.
C'MON--! GIVE US SOME MONEY!
THANK YOU VERY MUCH--
--BUT WE WON'T BE NEEDING ANY.

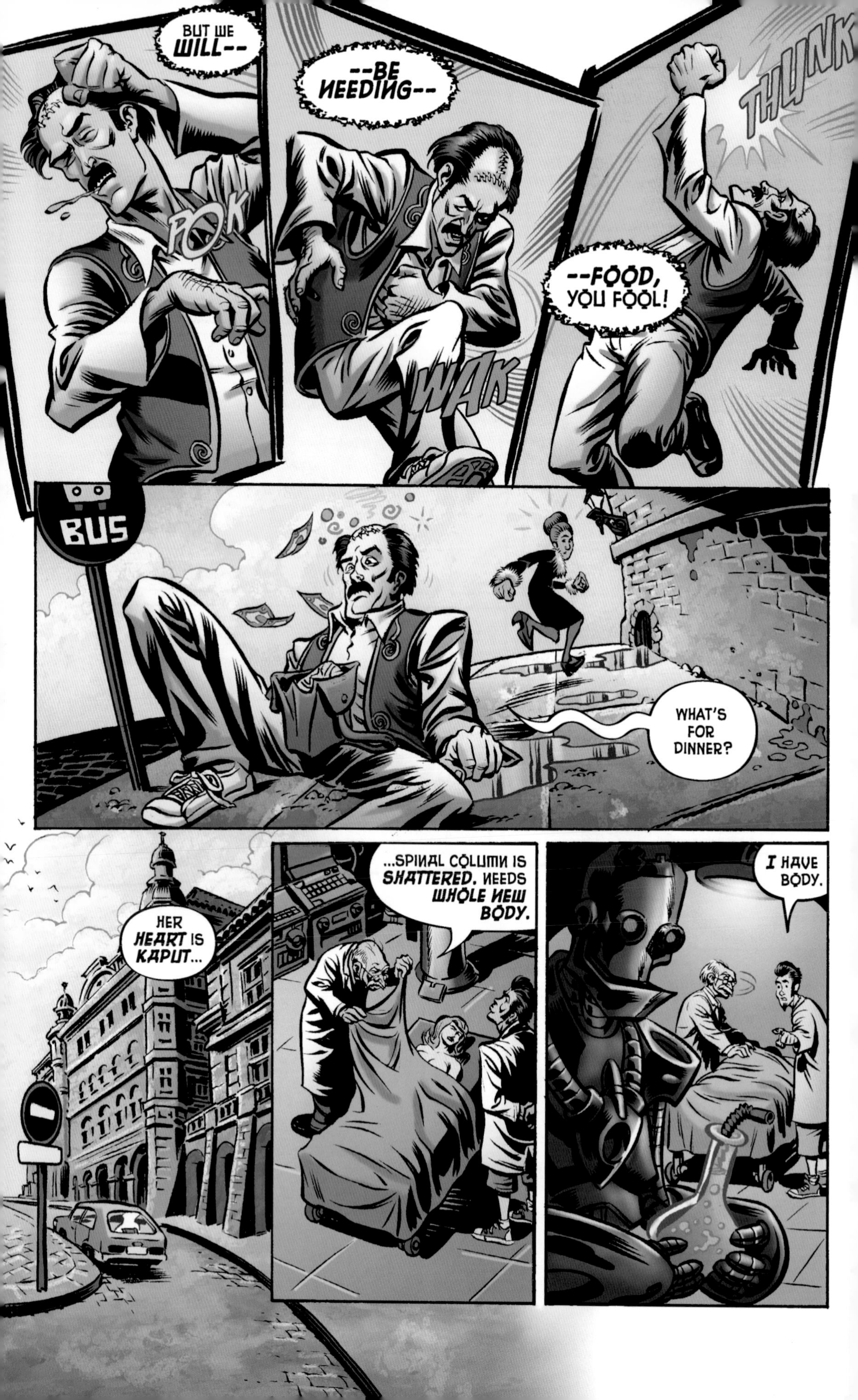
BUT WE WILL--
POK
--BE NEEDING--
WAK
THUNK
--FOOD, YOU FOOL!
BUS
WHAT'S FOR DINNER?
HER HEART IS KAPUT...
...SPINAL COLUMN IS SHATTERED. NEEDS WHOLE NEW BODY.
I HAVE BODY.

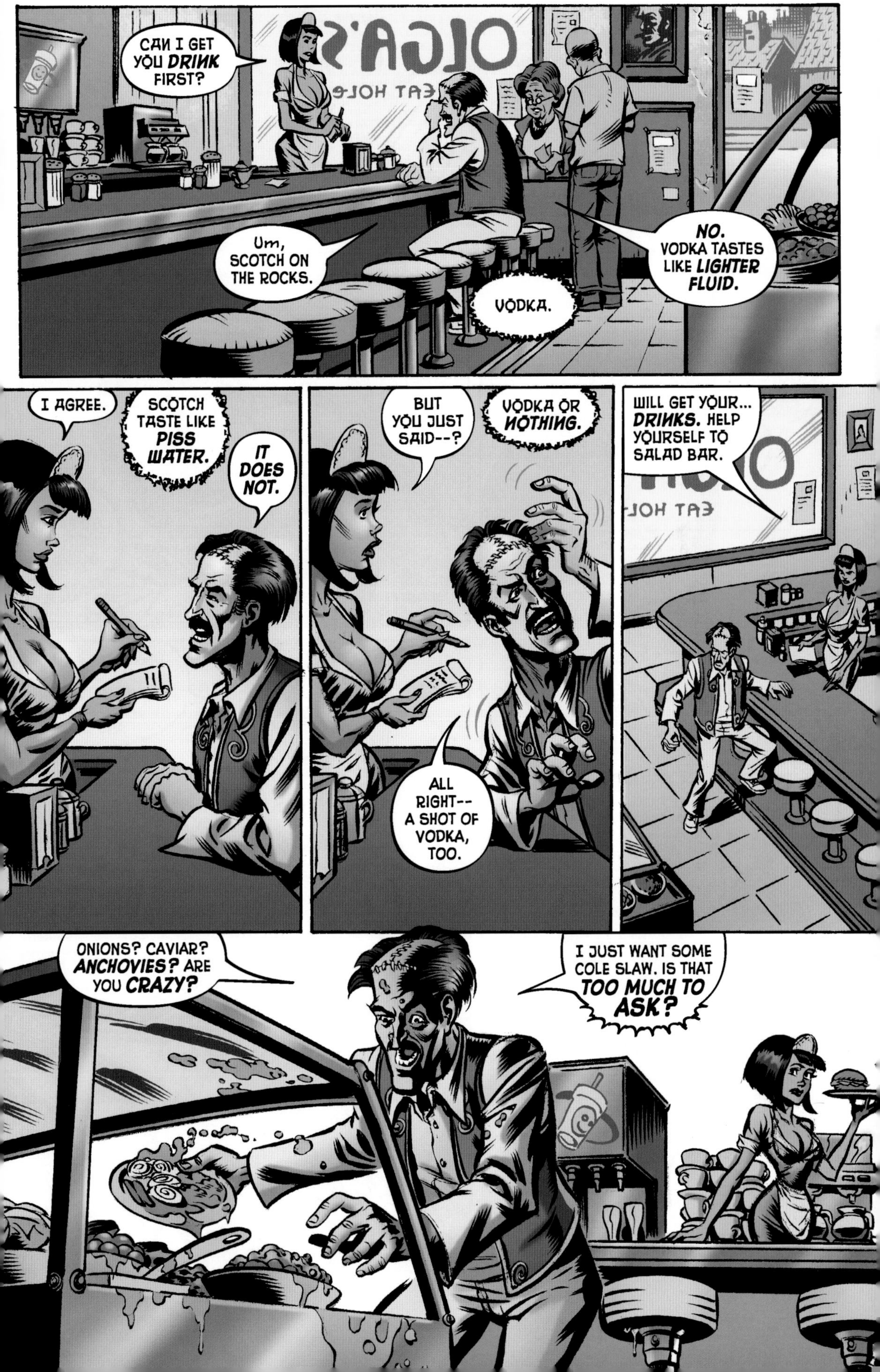
CAN I GET YOU DRINK FIRST?
OLGA'S EAT HOLE
Um, SCOTCH ON THE ROCKS.
VODKA.
NO. VODKA TASTES LIKE LIGHTER FLUID.
I AGREE.
SCOTCH TASTE LIKE PISS WATER.
IT DOES NOT.
BUT YOU JUST SAID--?
VODKA OR NOTHING.
ALL RIGHT-- A SHOT OF VODKA, TOO.
WILL GET YOUR... DRINKS. HELP YOURSELF TO SALAD BAR.
ONIONS? CAVIAR? ANCHOVIES? ARE YOU CRAZY?
I JUST WANT SOME COLE SLAW. IS THAT TOO MUCH TO ASK?

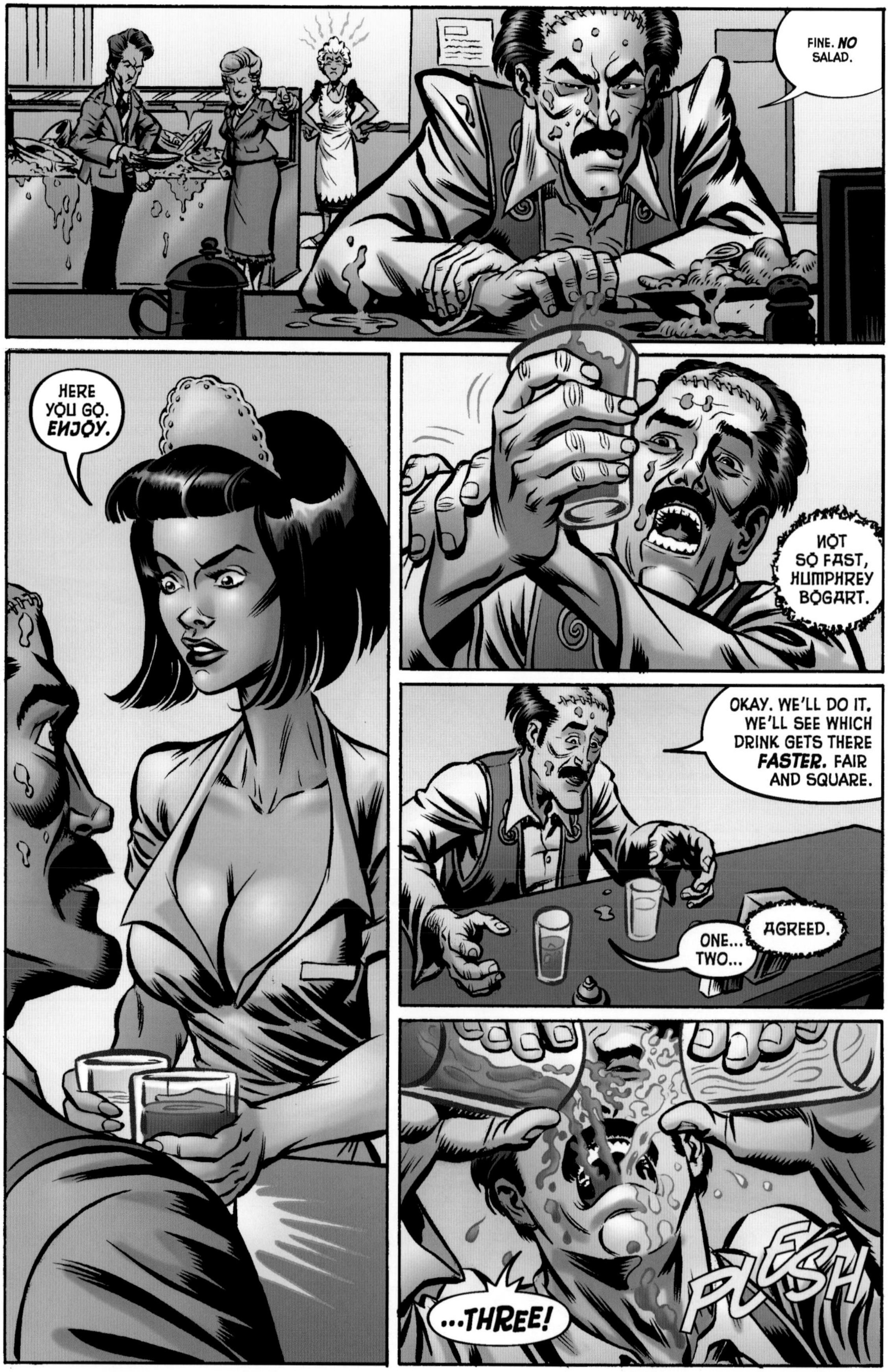
FINE. NO SALAD.
HERE YOU GO. ENJOY.
NOT SO FAST, HUMPHREY BOGART.
OKAY. WE'LL DO IT. WE'LL SEE WHICH DRINK GETS THERE FASTER. FAIR AND SQUARE.
AGREED.
ONE... TWO...
...THREE!
PLESH

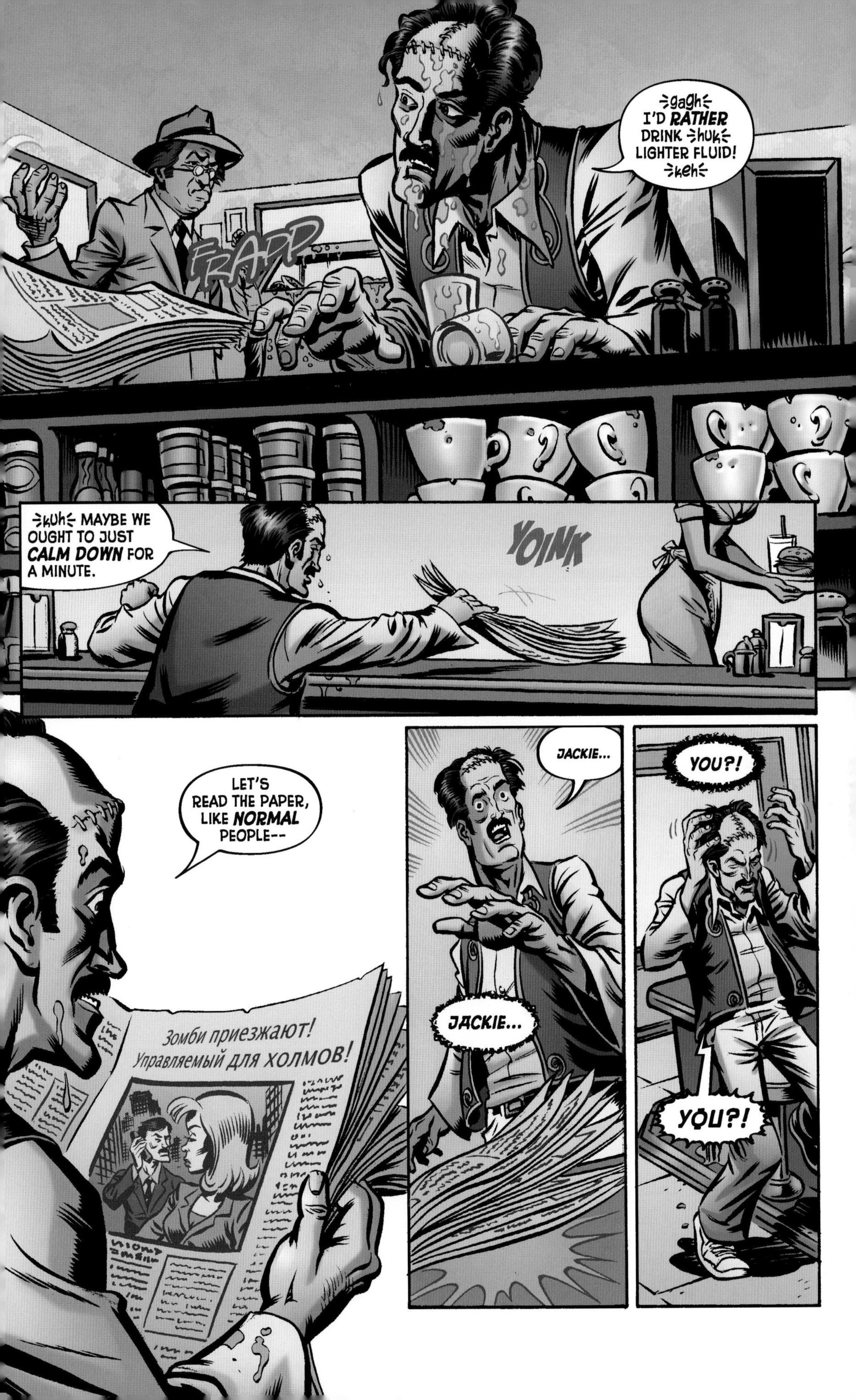
FRAPP
gagh I'D RATHER DRINK huk LIGHTER FLUID! keh
kuh MAYBE WE OUGHT TO JUST CALM DOWN FOR A MINUTE.
YOINK
LET'S READ THE PAPER, LIKE NORMAL PEOPLE--
Зомби приезжают!
Управляемый для холмов!
JACKIE...
JACKIE...
YOU?!
YOU?!

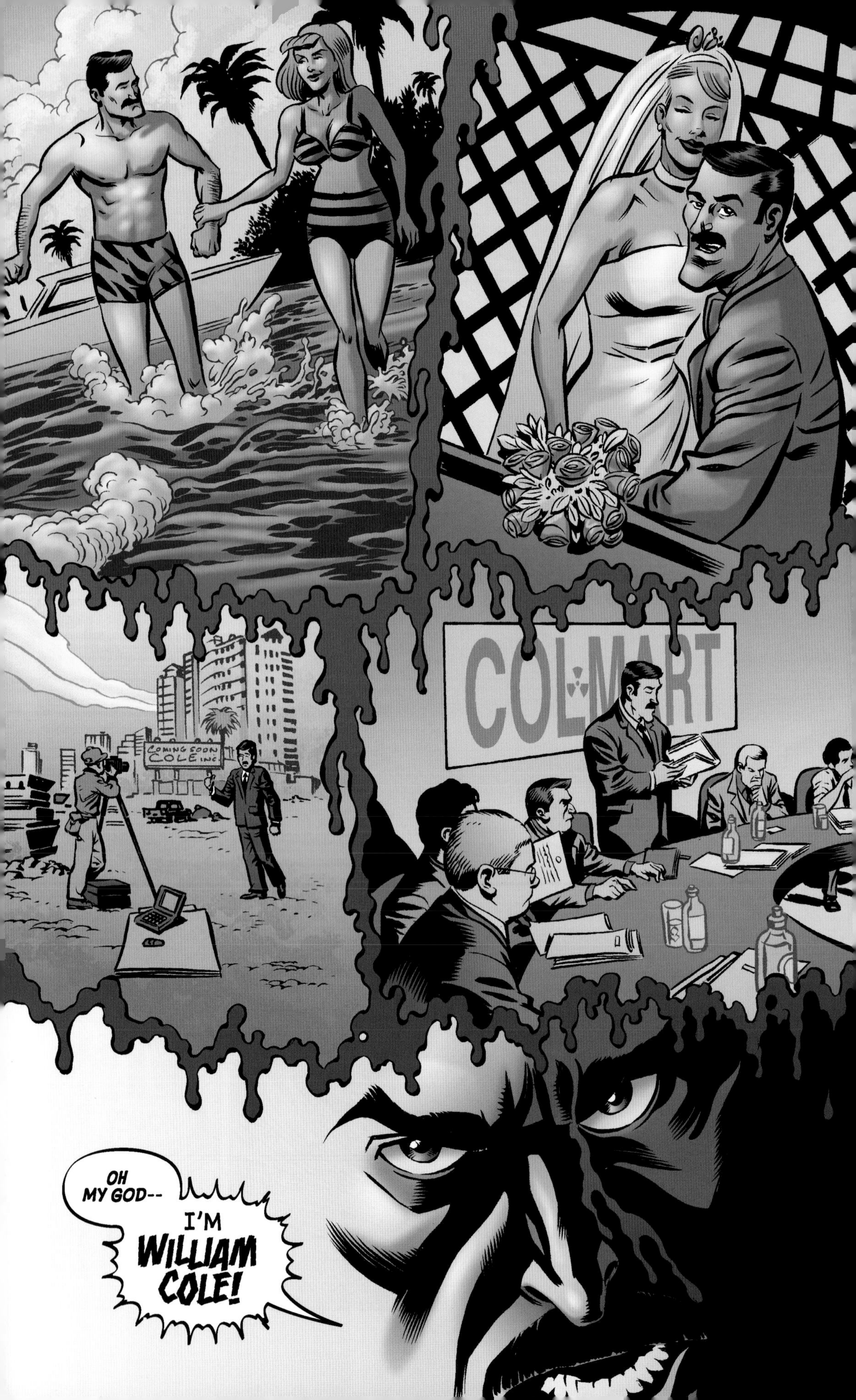
COLMART
COMING SOON
COLE INC.
OH MY GOD--
I'M WILLIAM COLE!

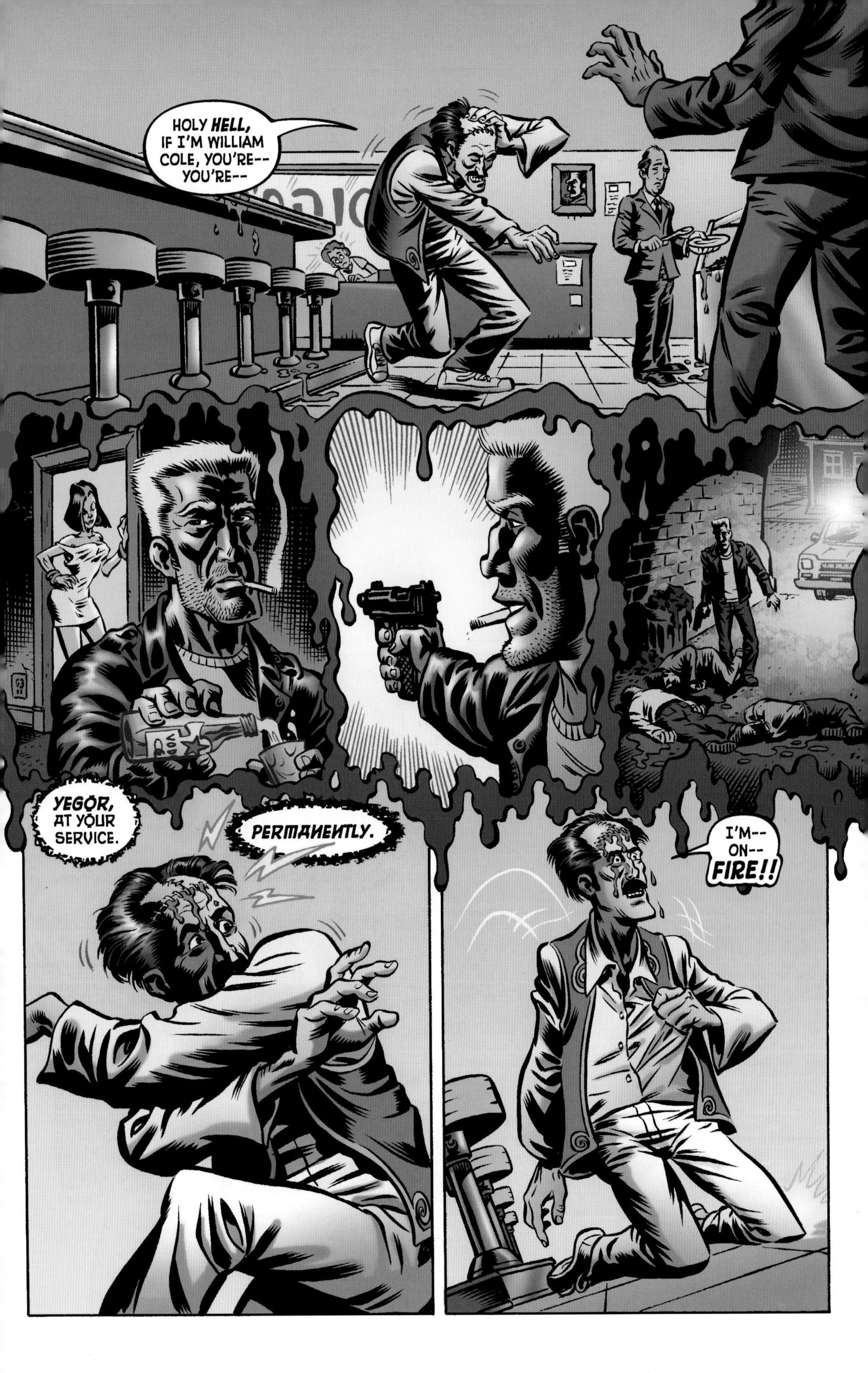
HOLY HELL, IF I'M WILLIAM COLE, YOU'RE-- YOU'RE--
YEGOR, AT YOUR SERVICE.
PERMANENTLY.
I'M-- ON-- FIRE!!

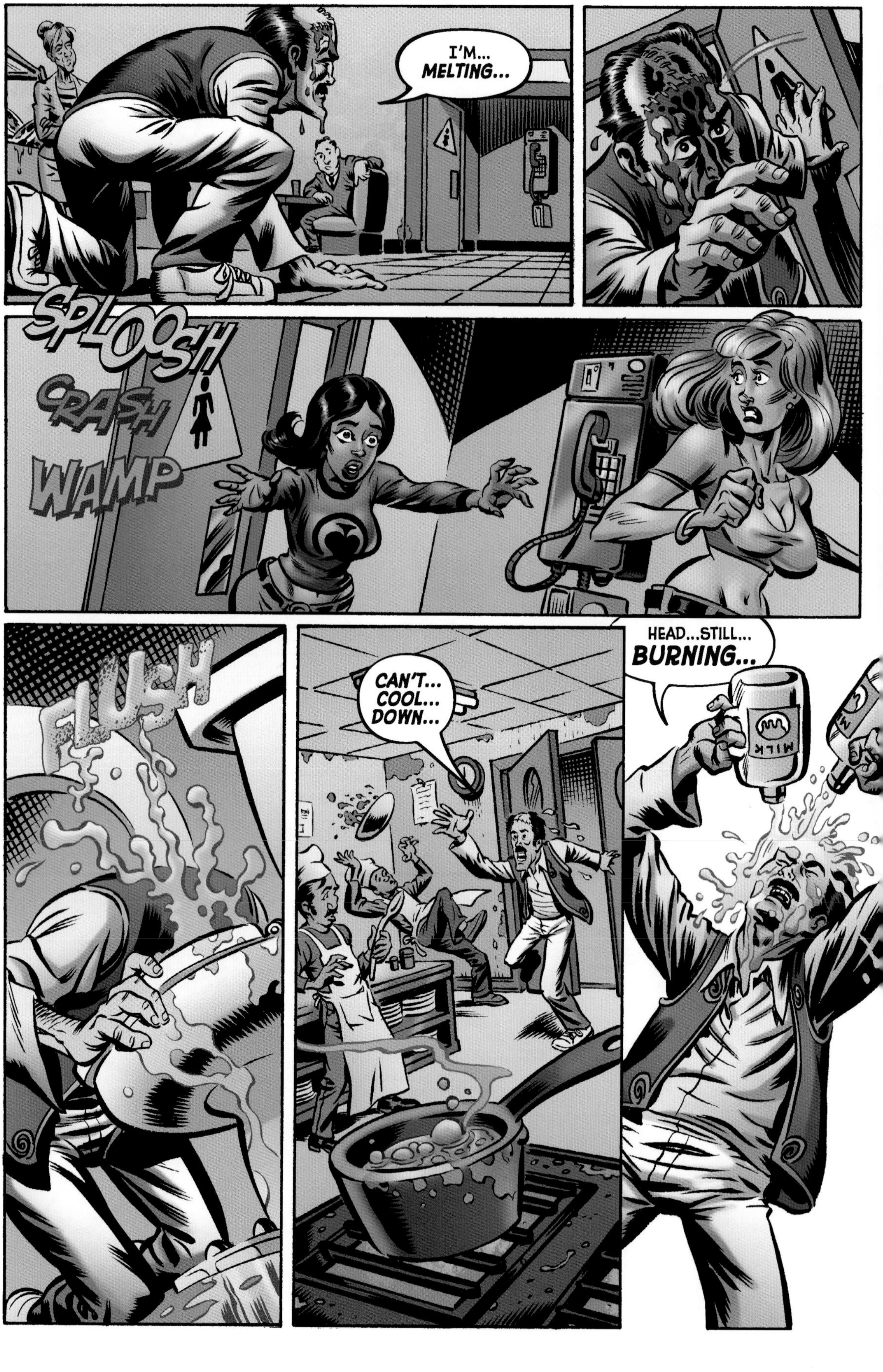

I'M...
MELTING...
SPLOOSH
CRASH
WAMP
FLUSH
CAN'T...
COOL...
DOWN...
HEAD...STILL...
BURNING...
MILK

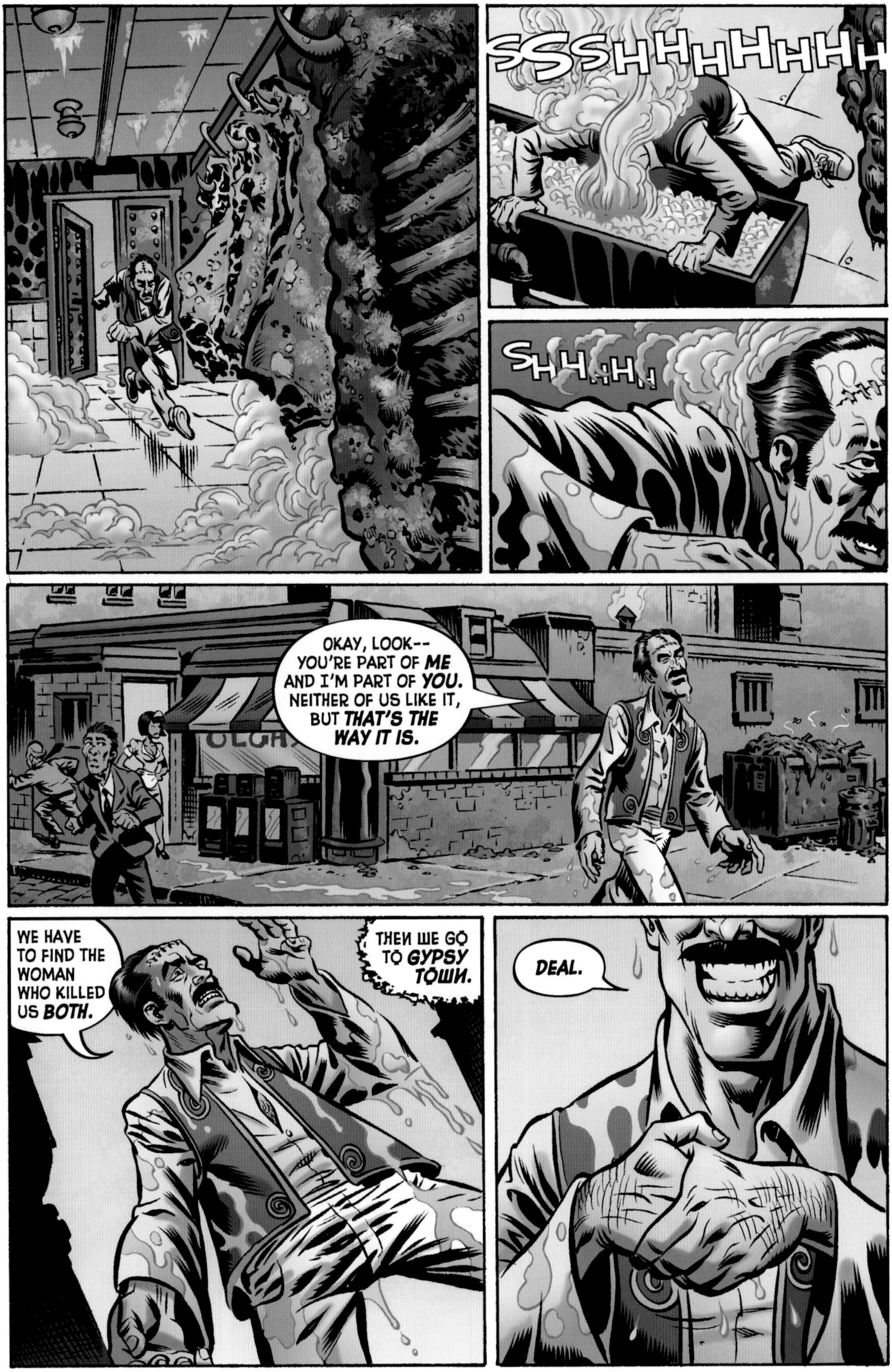
SSSHHHHHHHH
SHHHHH
OKAY, LOOK-- YOU'RE PART OF ME AND I'M PART OF YOU. NEITHER OF US LIKE IT, BUT THAT'S THE WAY IT IS.
WE HAVE TO FIND THE WOMAN WHO KILLED US BOTH.
THEN WE GO TO GYPSY TOWN.
DEAL.

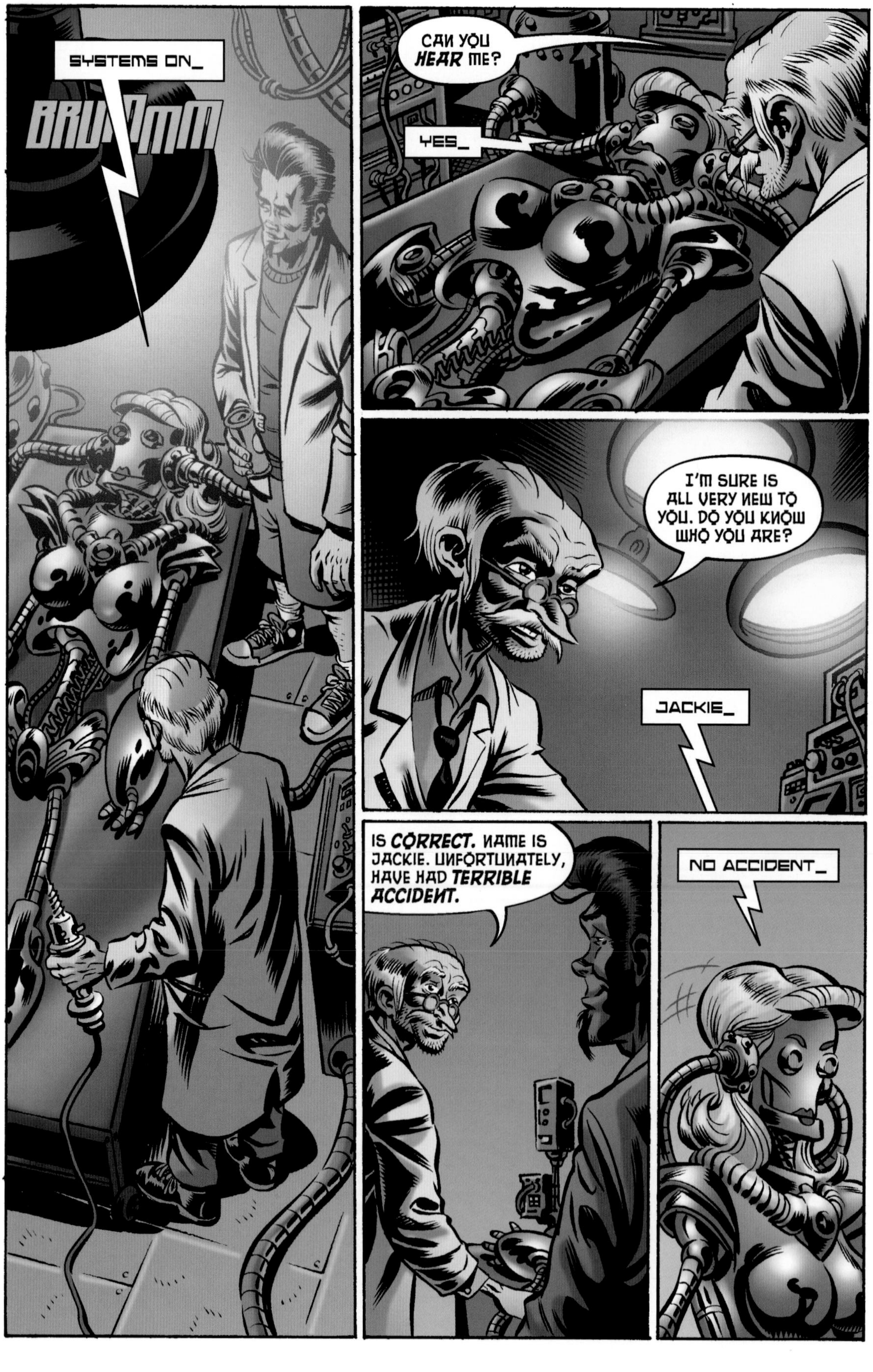
SYSTEMS ON_
BRUMMM
CAN YOU HEAR ME?
YES_
I'M SURE IS ALL VERY NEW TO YOU. DO YOU KNOW WHO YOU ARE?
JACKIE_
IS CORRECT. NAME IS JACKIE. UNFORTUNATELY, HAVE HAD TERRIBLE ACCIDENT.
NO ACCIDENT_

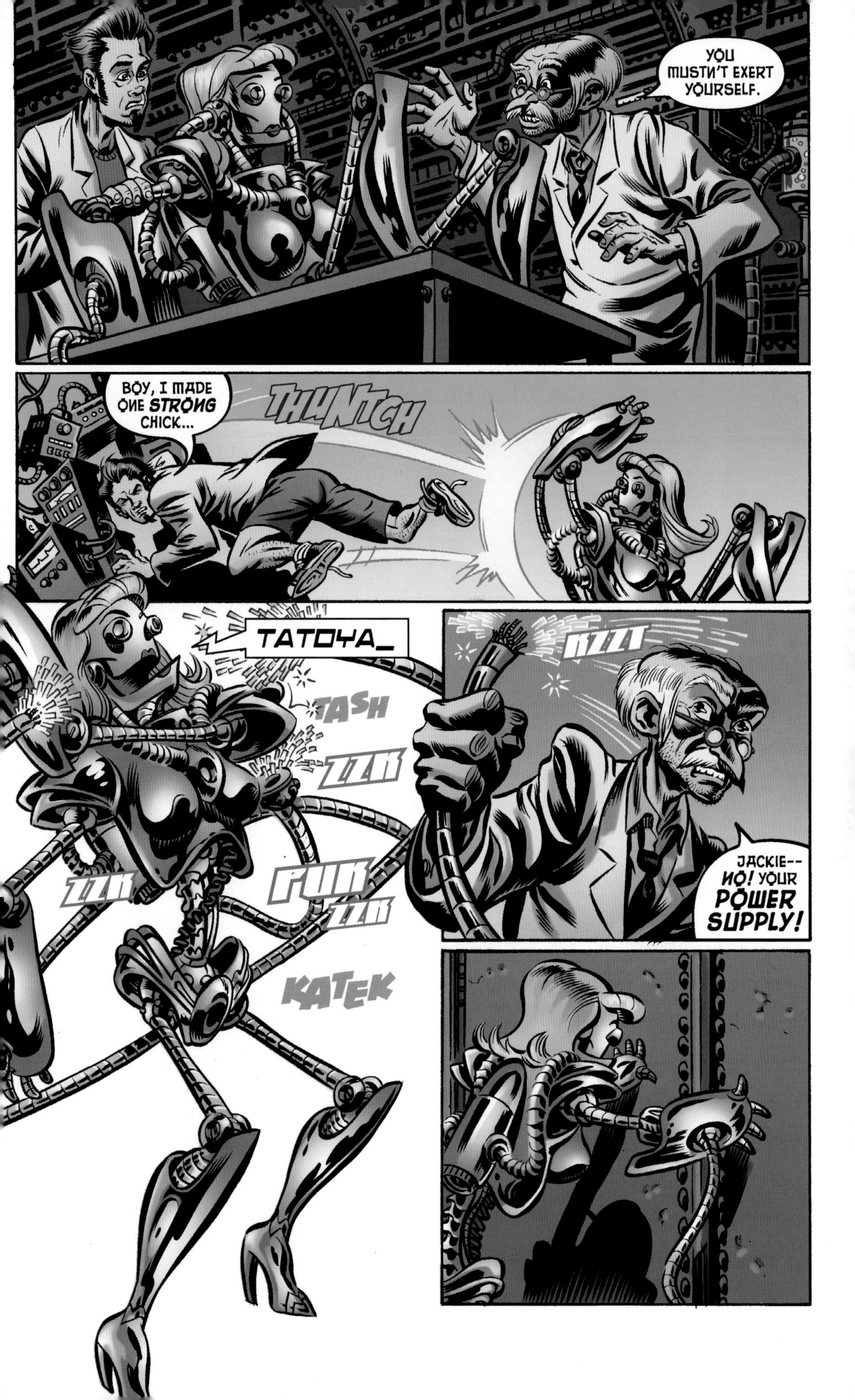
YOU MUSTN'T EXERT YOURSELF.
BOY, I MADE ONE STRONG CHICK...
THUNTCH
TATOYA_
TASH
ZZZK
ZZZK
PUK
ZZZK
KATEK
KZZZT
JACKIE-- NO! YOUR POWER SUPPLY!

GYPSY TOWN_

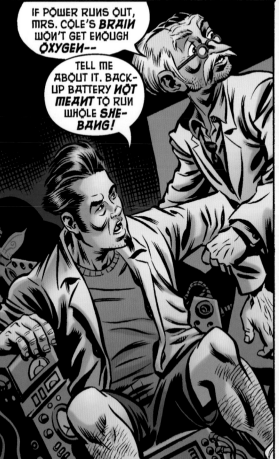

IF POWER RUNS OUT, MRS. COLE'S *BRAIN* WON'T GET ENOUGH *OXYGEN*--

TELL ME ABOUT IT. BACK-UP BATTERY *NOT MEANT* TO RUN WHOLE *SHE-BANG!*

BRING HER BACK, PAVEL--AND *WILLIAM COLE,* ALSO!

YES, YES ...

...AND IN *SPARE TIME,* RELIEVE *WORLD HUNGER...*

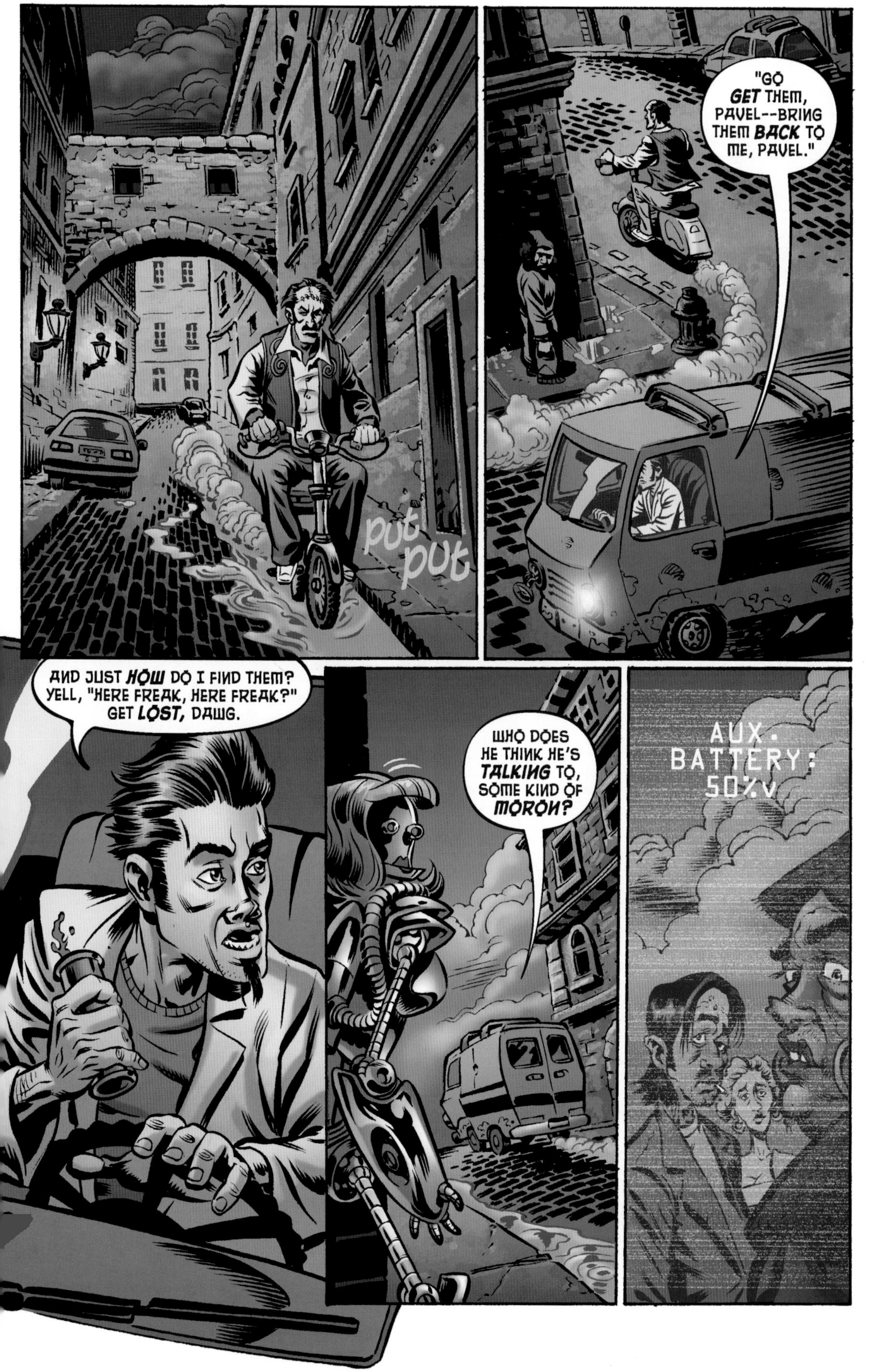
put
put
"GO GET THEM, PAVEL--BRING THEM BACK TO ME, PAVEL."
AND JUST HOW DO I FIND THEM? YELL, "HERE FREAK, HERE FREAK?" GET LOST, DAWG.
WHO DOES HE THINK HE'S TALKING TO, SOME KIND OF MORON?
AUX. BATTERY: 50%v

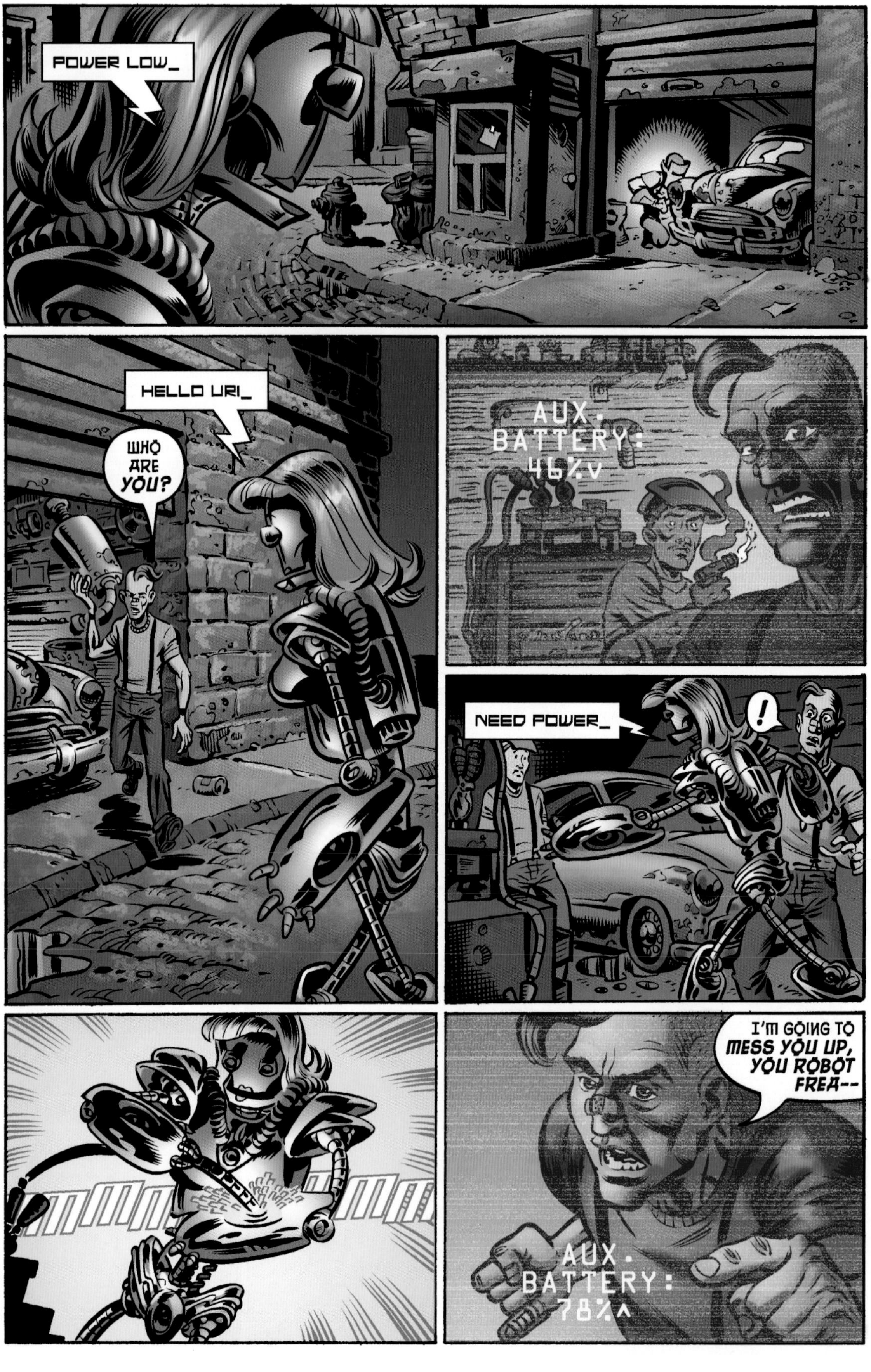
POWER LOW_
HELLO URI_
WHO ARE YOU?
AUX. BATTERY: 46%v
NEED POWER_
!
I'M GOING TO MESS YOU UP, YOU ROBOT FREA--
AUX. BATTERY: 78%^

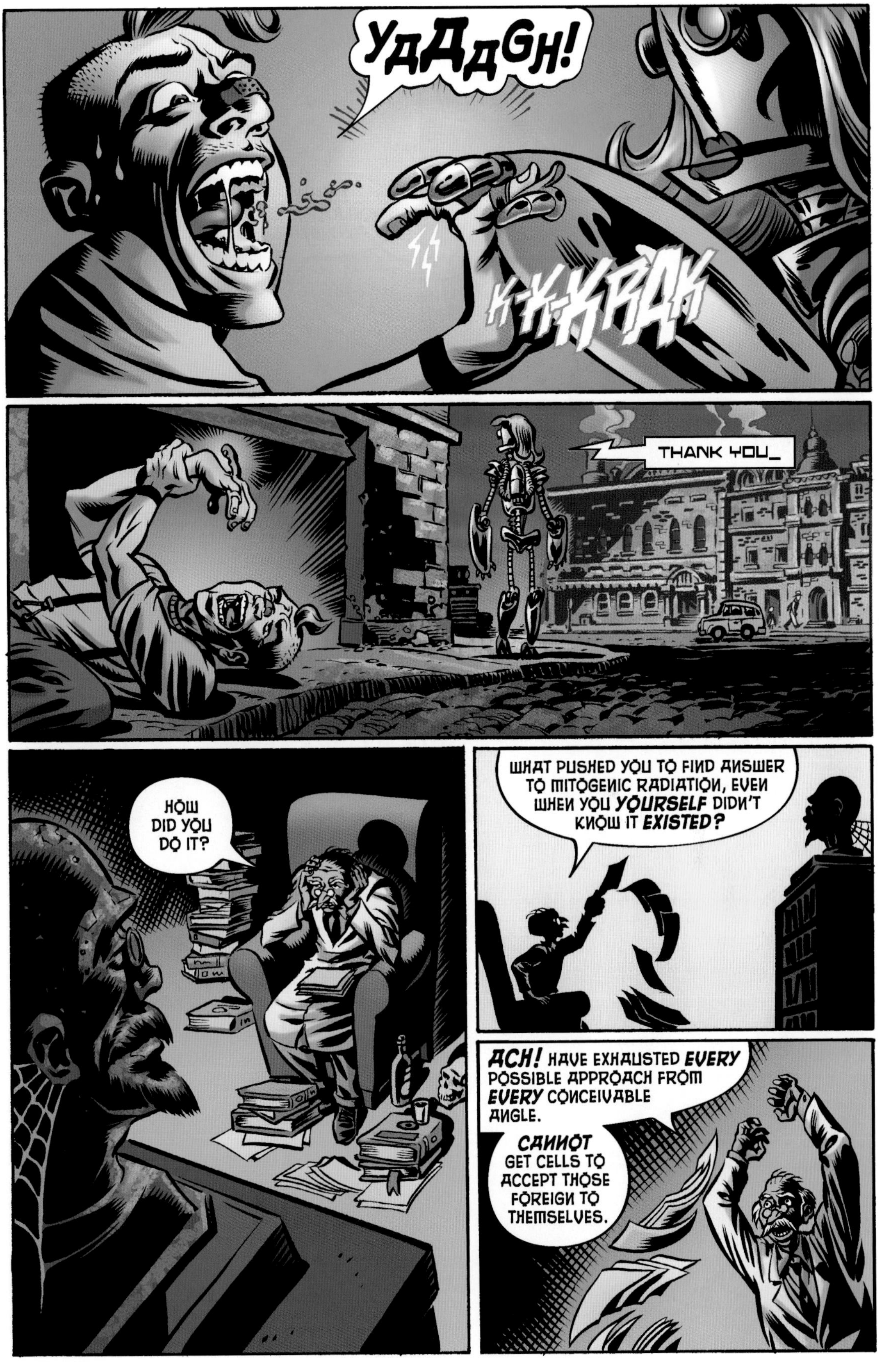
YAAAGH!
K-K-KRAK
THANK YOU_
HOW DID YOU DO IT?
WHAT PUSHED YOU TO FIND ANSWER TO MITOGENIC RADIATION, EVEN WHEN YOU YOURSELF DIDN'T KNOW IT EXISTED?
ACH! HAVE EXHAUSTED EVERY POSSIBLE APPROACH FROM EVERY CONCEIVABLE ANGLE.
CANNOT GET CELLS TO ACCEPT THOSE FOREIGN TO THEMSELVES.

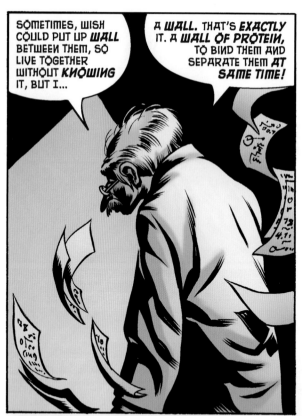

SOMETIMES, WISH COULD PUT UP *WALL* BETWEEN THEM, SO LIVE TOGETHER WITHOUT *KNOWING* IT, BUT I...

A *WALL.* THAT'S *EXACTLY* IT. A *WALL OF PROTEIN,* TO BIND THEM AND SEPARATE THEM *AT SAME TIME!*

THANK YOU, COMRADE ALEXANDER.

ANYONE OBJECT, SPEAK *NOW...*

...OR *FOREVER HOLD YOUR PEACE.*

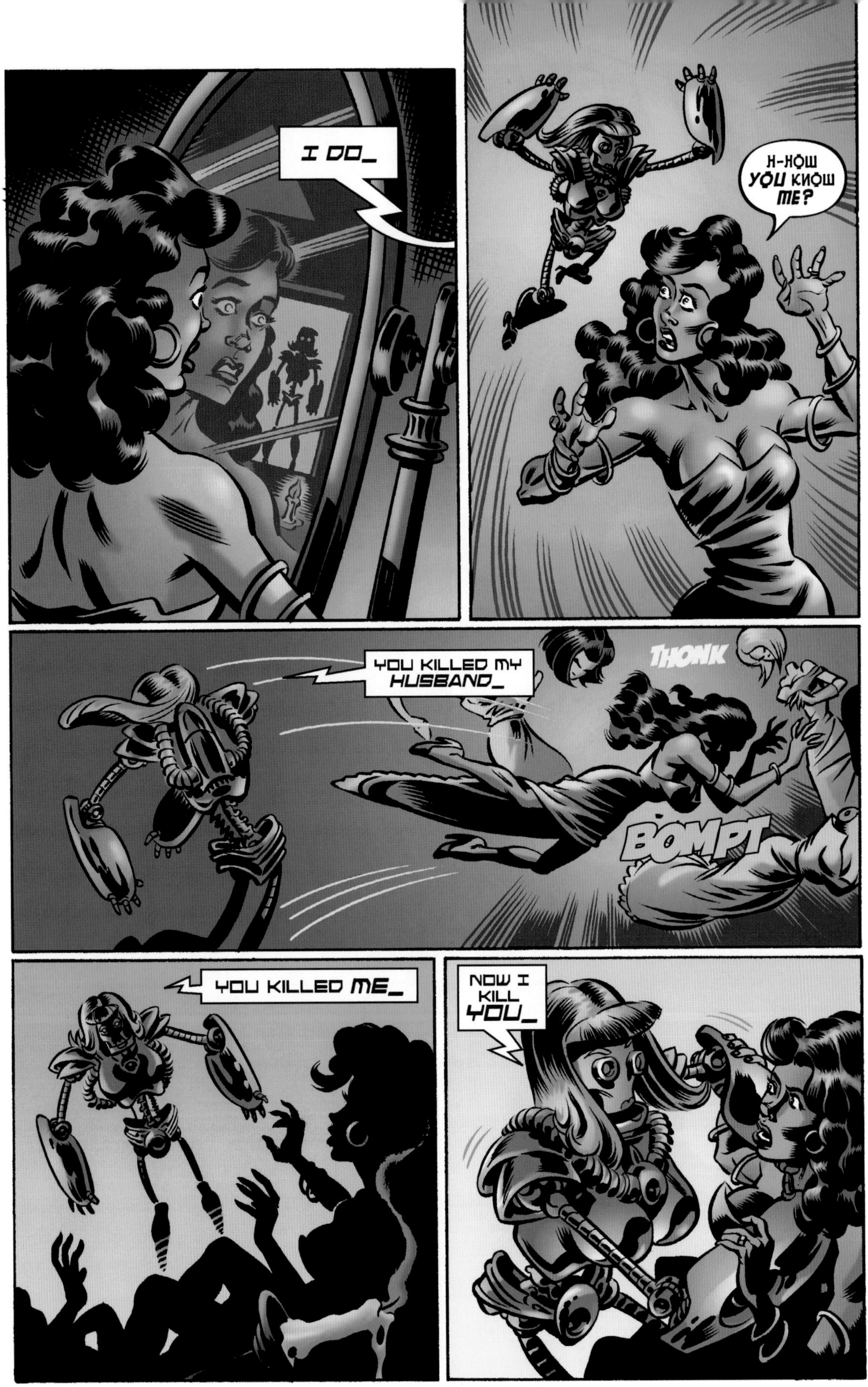

I DO_
H-HOW YOU KNOW ME?
YOU KILLED MY HUSBAND_
THONK
BOMPT
YOU KILLED ME_
NOW I KILL YOU_

BAM

CHKK

RZZ
PUK
PAFF

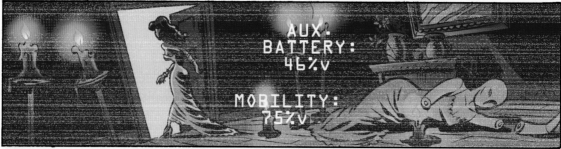

AUX-
BATTERY:
46%v

MOBILITY:
75%v

IT'S
HER!

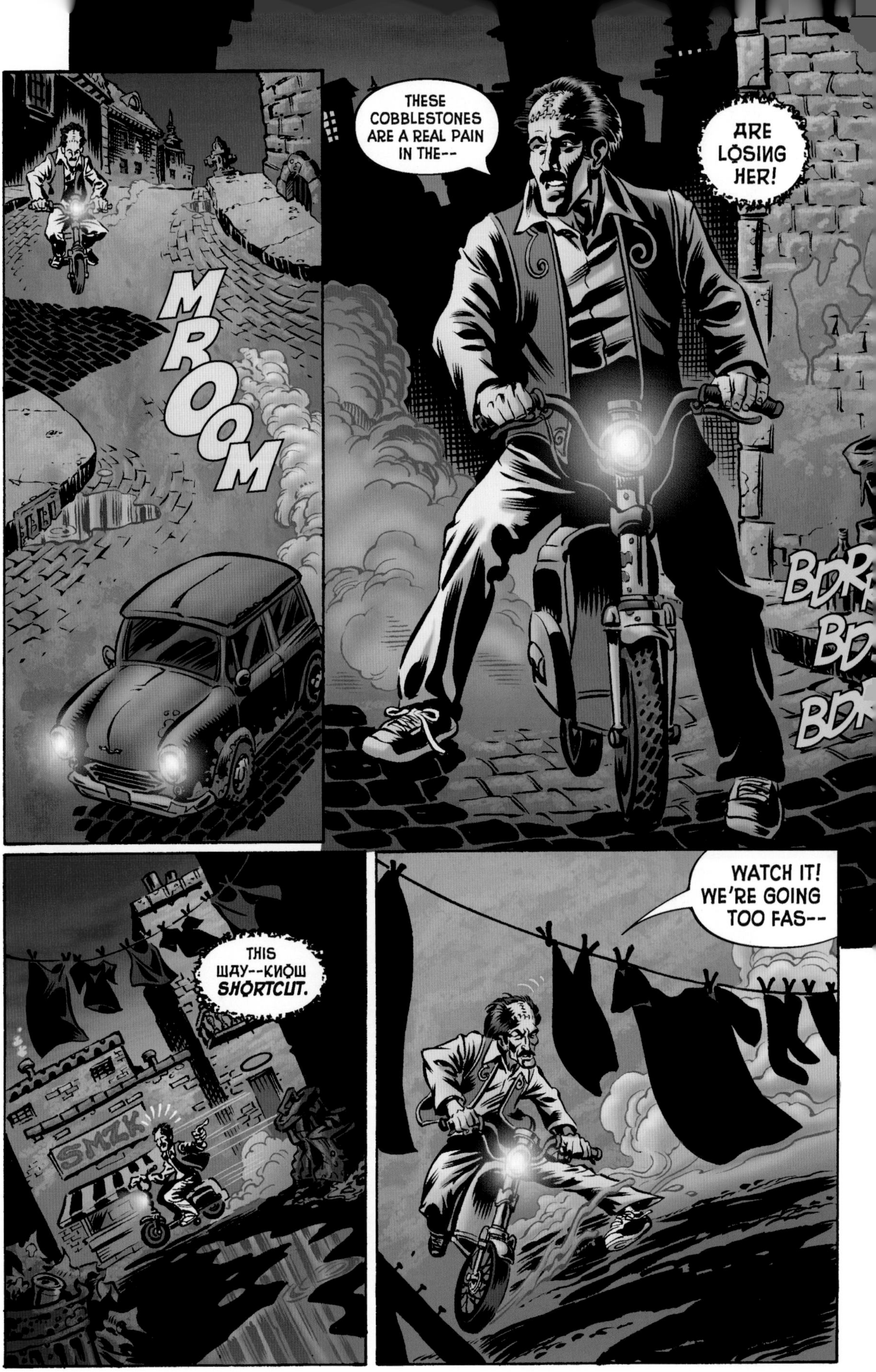

MROOM
THESE COBBLESTONES ARE A REAL PAIN IN THE--
ARE LOSING HER!
THIS WAY--KNOW SHORTCUT.
SMZK
WATCH IT! WE'RE GOING TOO FAS--

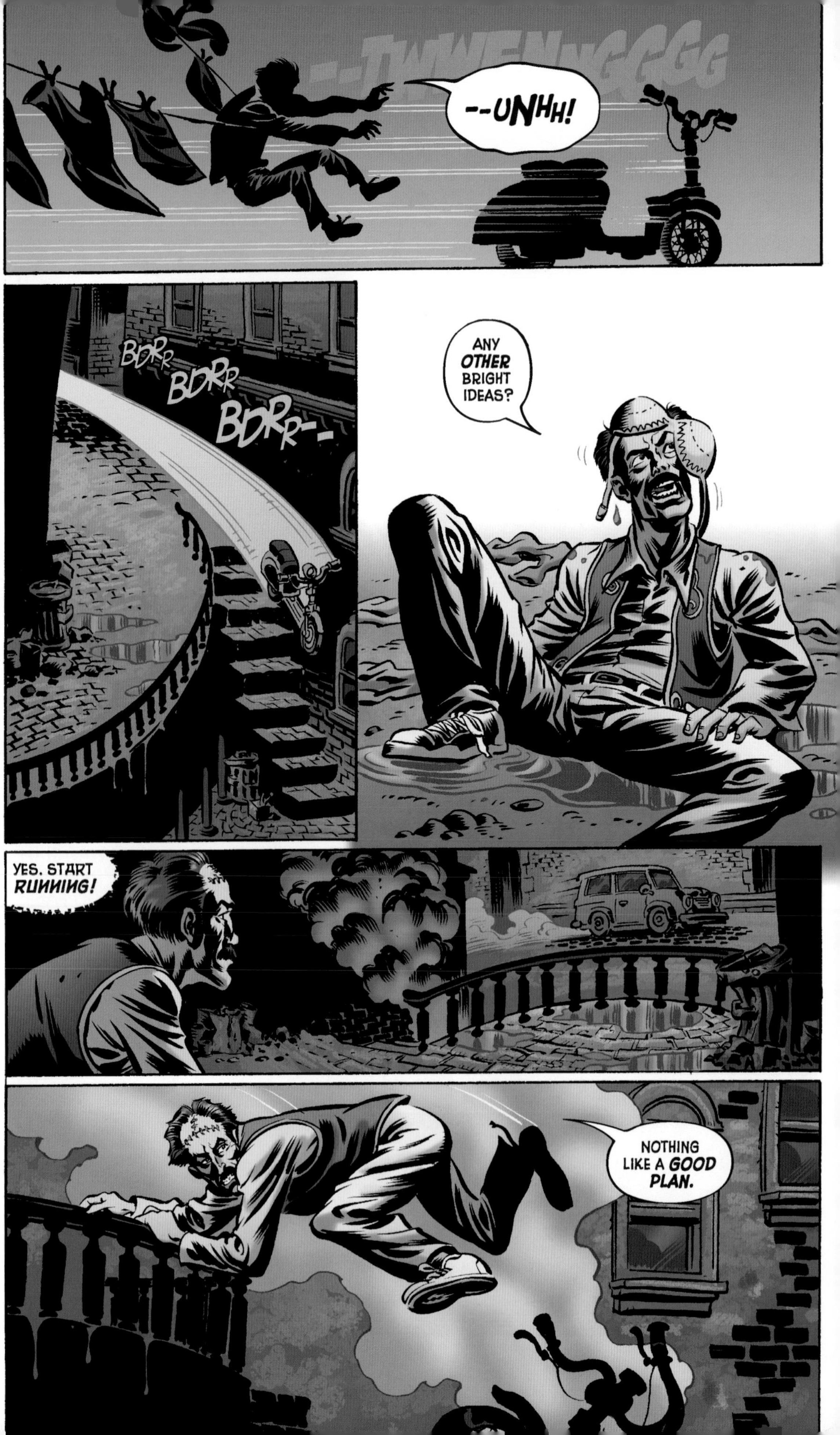
--TWWENNGGGG
--UNHH!
BDRR
BDRR
BDRR--
ANY OTHER BRIGHT IDEAS?
YES. START RUNNING!
NOTHING LIKE A GOOD PLAN.

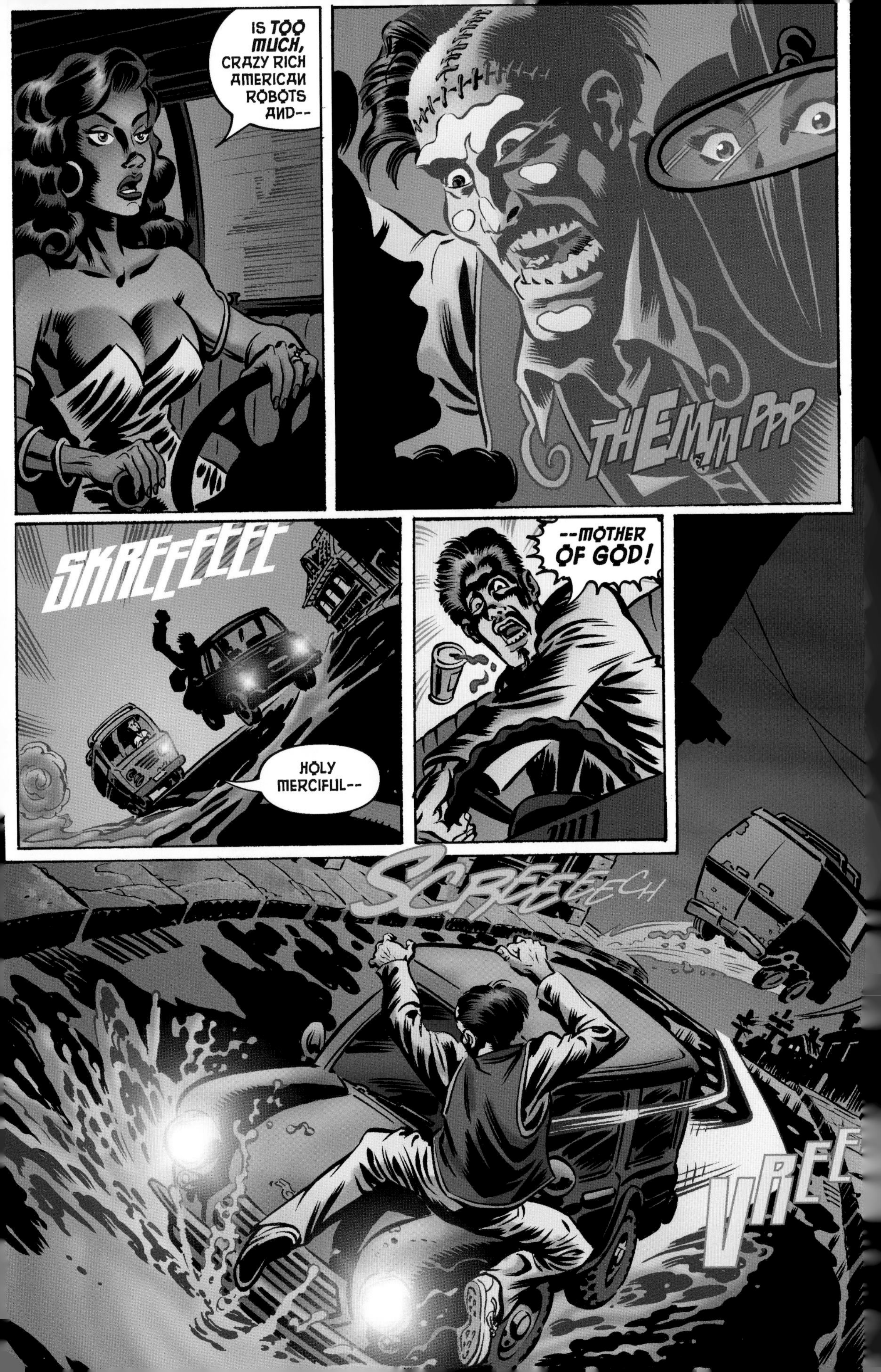
IS TOO MUCH, CRAZY RICH AMERICAN ROBOTS AND--
THEMMPPP
SKREEEEEE
HOLY MERCIFUL--
--MOTHER OF GOD!
SCREEEEECH
VREE

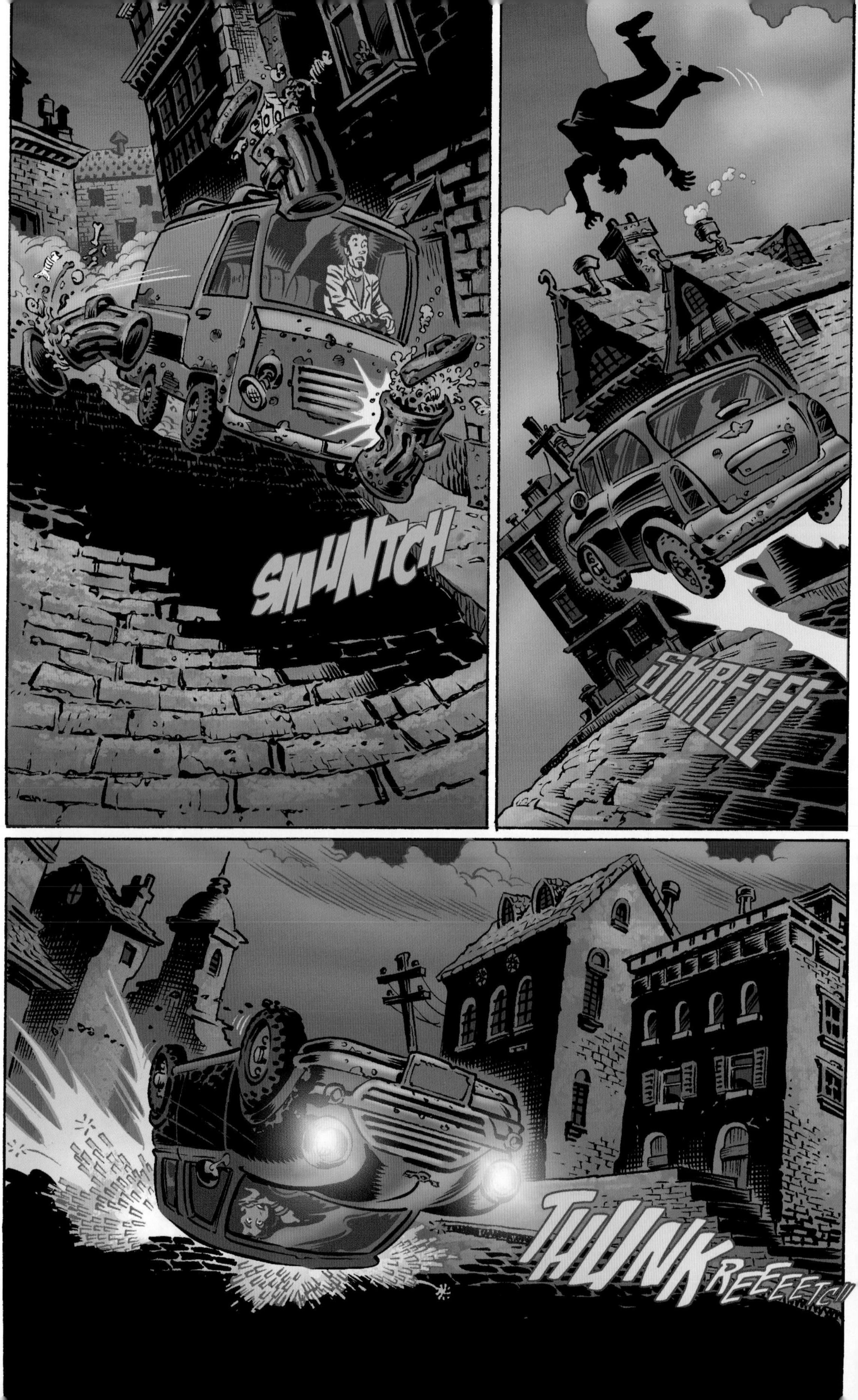
SMUNTCH
SKREEEE
THUNK
REEEEETCH!!

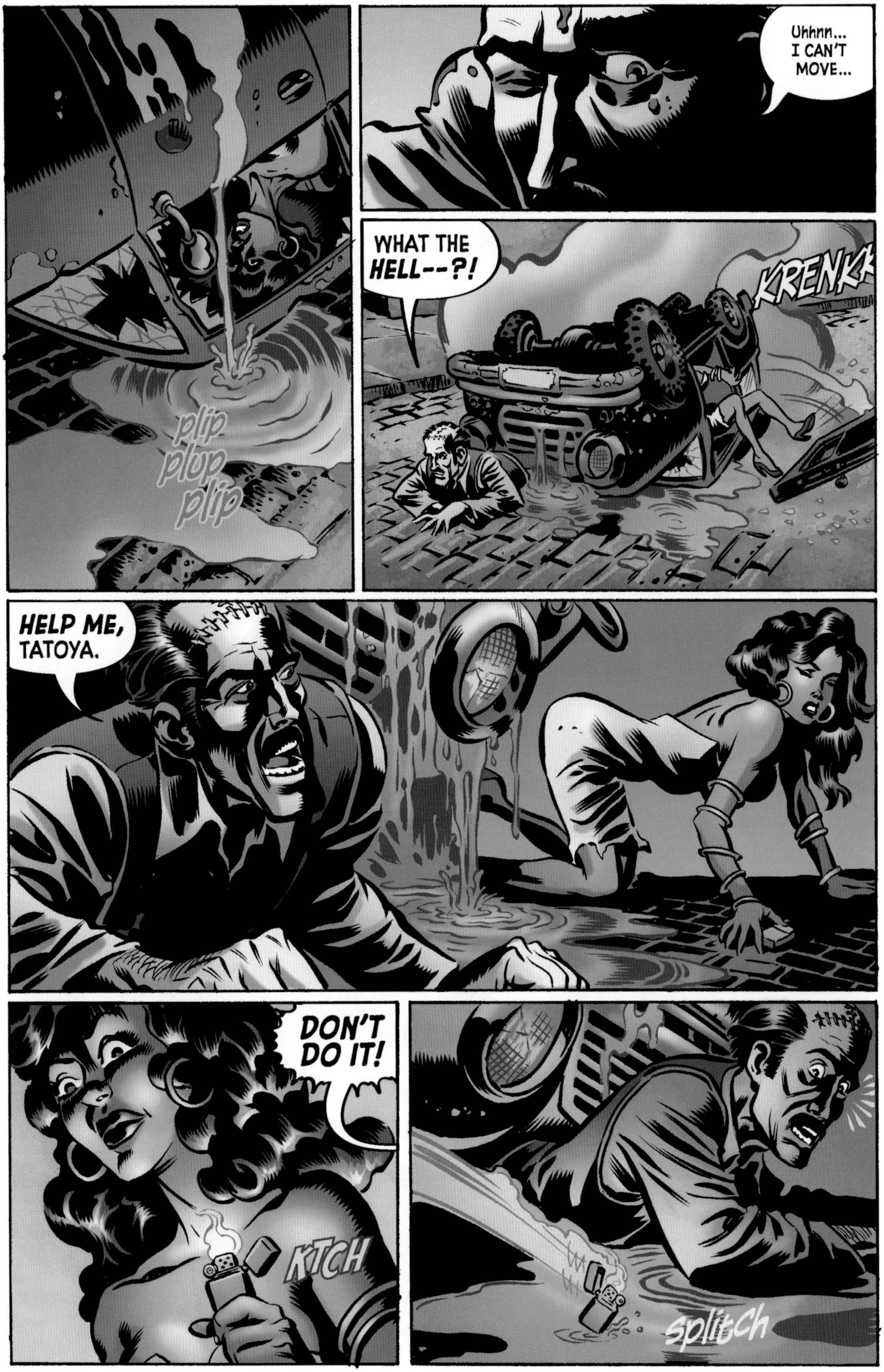
plip
plup
plip
Uhhnn... I CAN'T MOVE...
WHAT THE HELL--?!
KRENKK
HELP ME, TATOYA.
DON'T DO IT!
KTCH
splitch

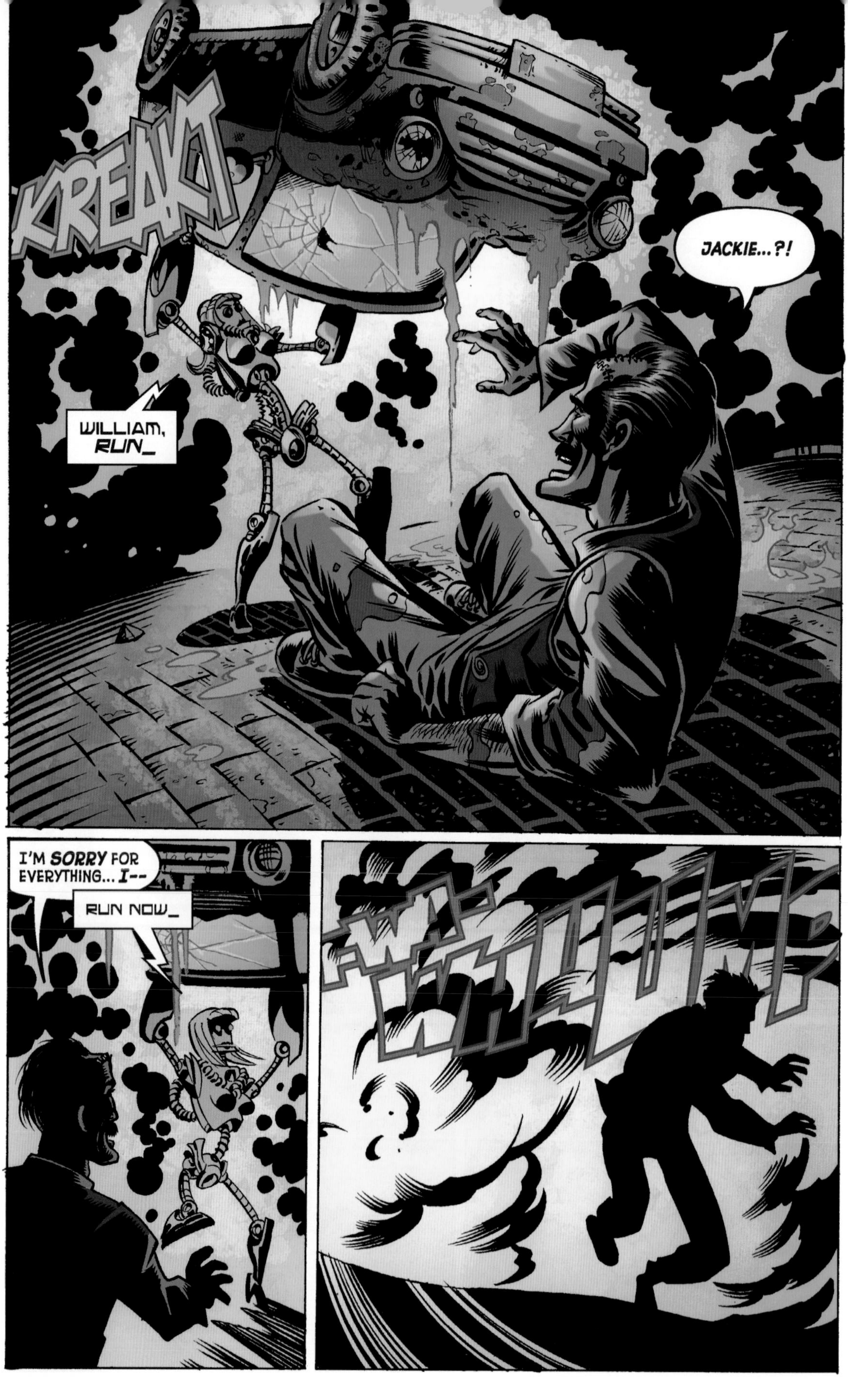
KREAK!
JACKIE...?!
WILLIAM, RUN_
I'M SORRY FOR EVERYTHING... I--
RUN NOW_

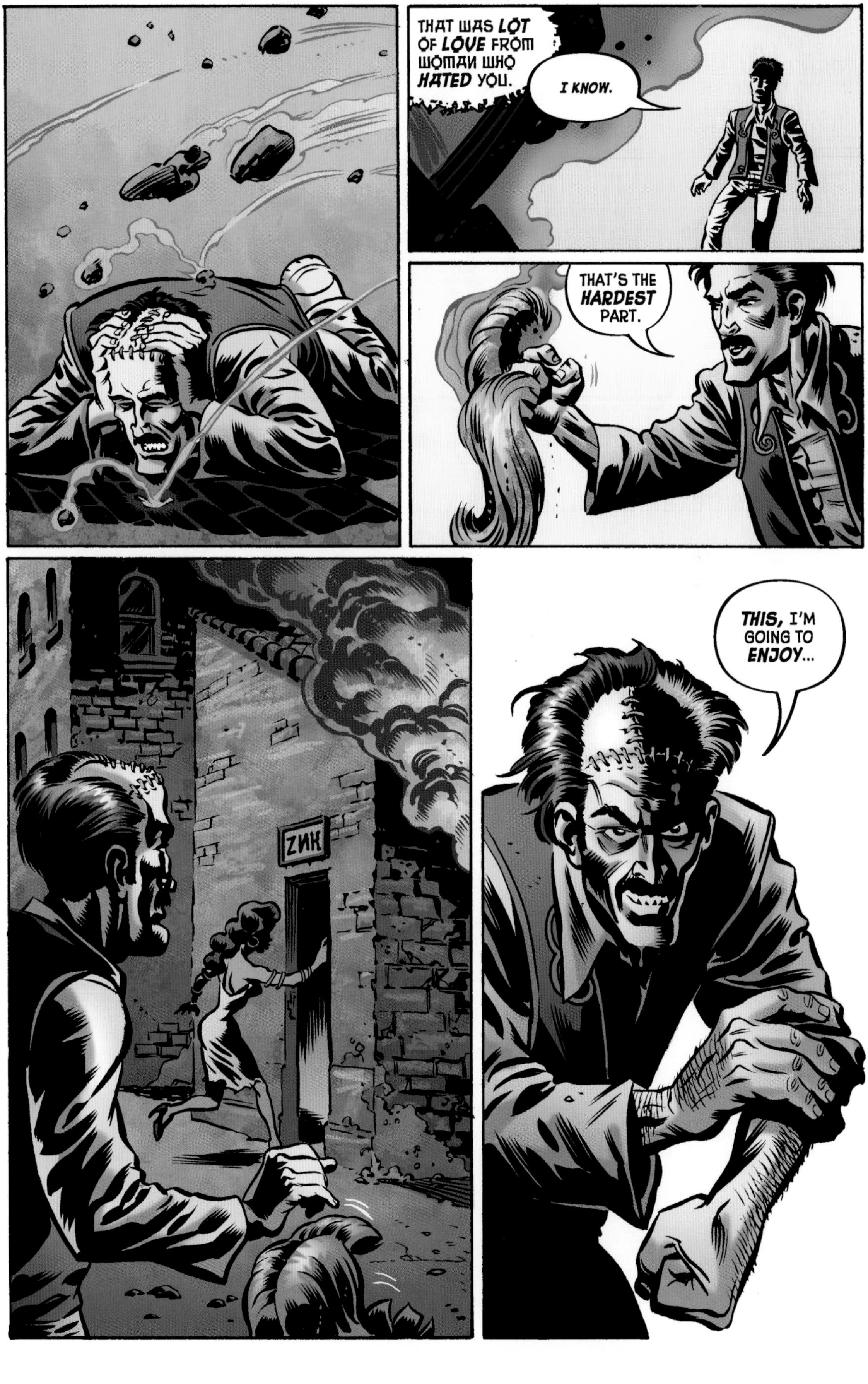
THAT WAS LOT OF LOVE FROM WOMAN WHO HATED YOU.
I KNOW.
THAT'S THE HARDEST PART.
ZNK
THIS, I'M GOING TO ENJOY...

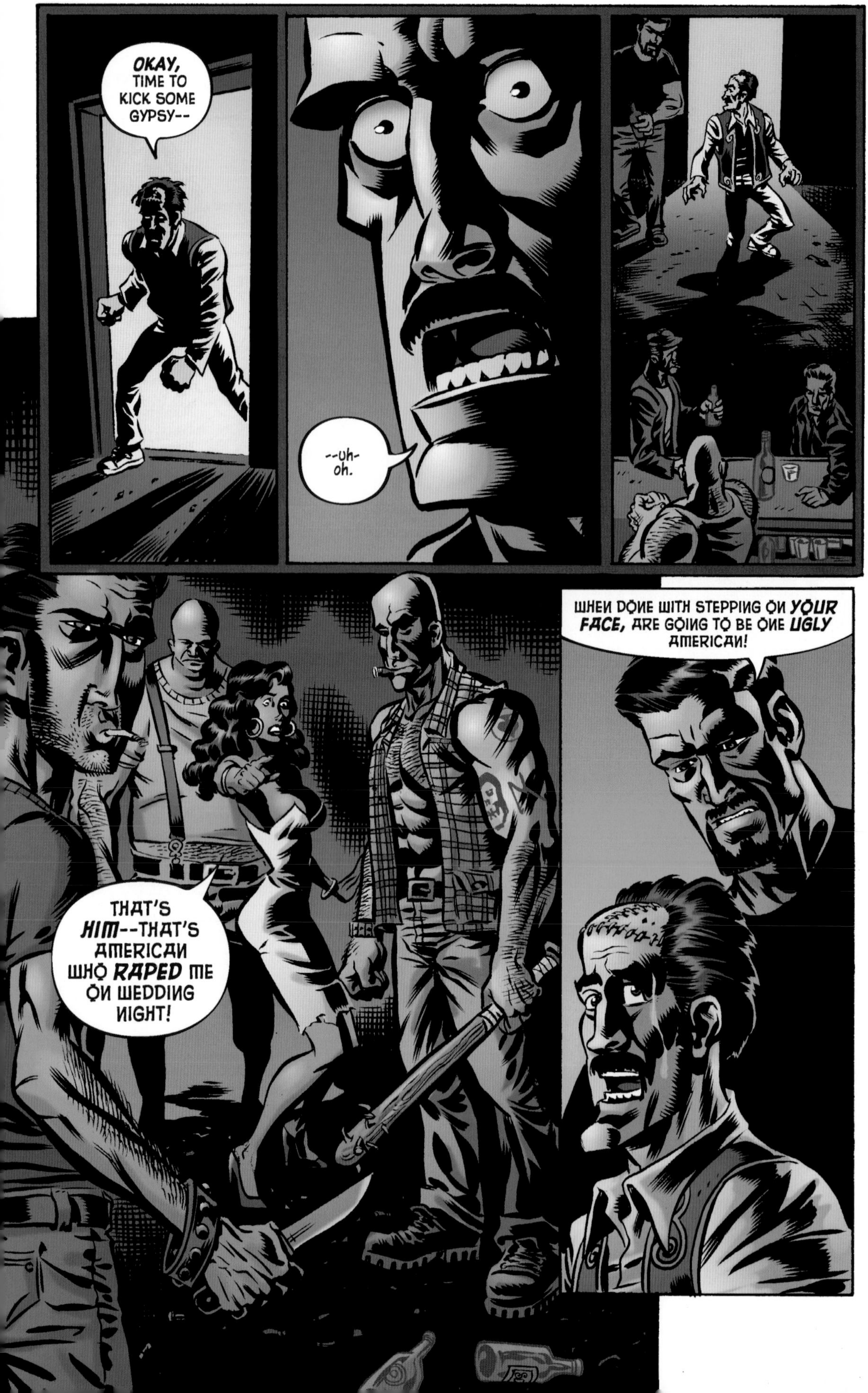
OKAY, TIME TO KICK SOME GYPSY--
--uh-oh.
WHEN DONE WITH STEPPING ON YOUR FACE, ARE GOING TO BE ONE UGLY AMERICAN!
THAT'S HIM--THAT'S AMERICAN WHO RAPED ME ON WEDDING NIGHT!

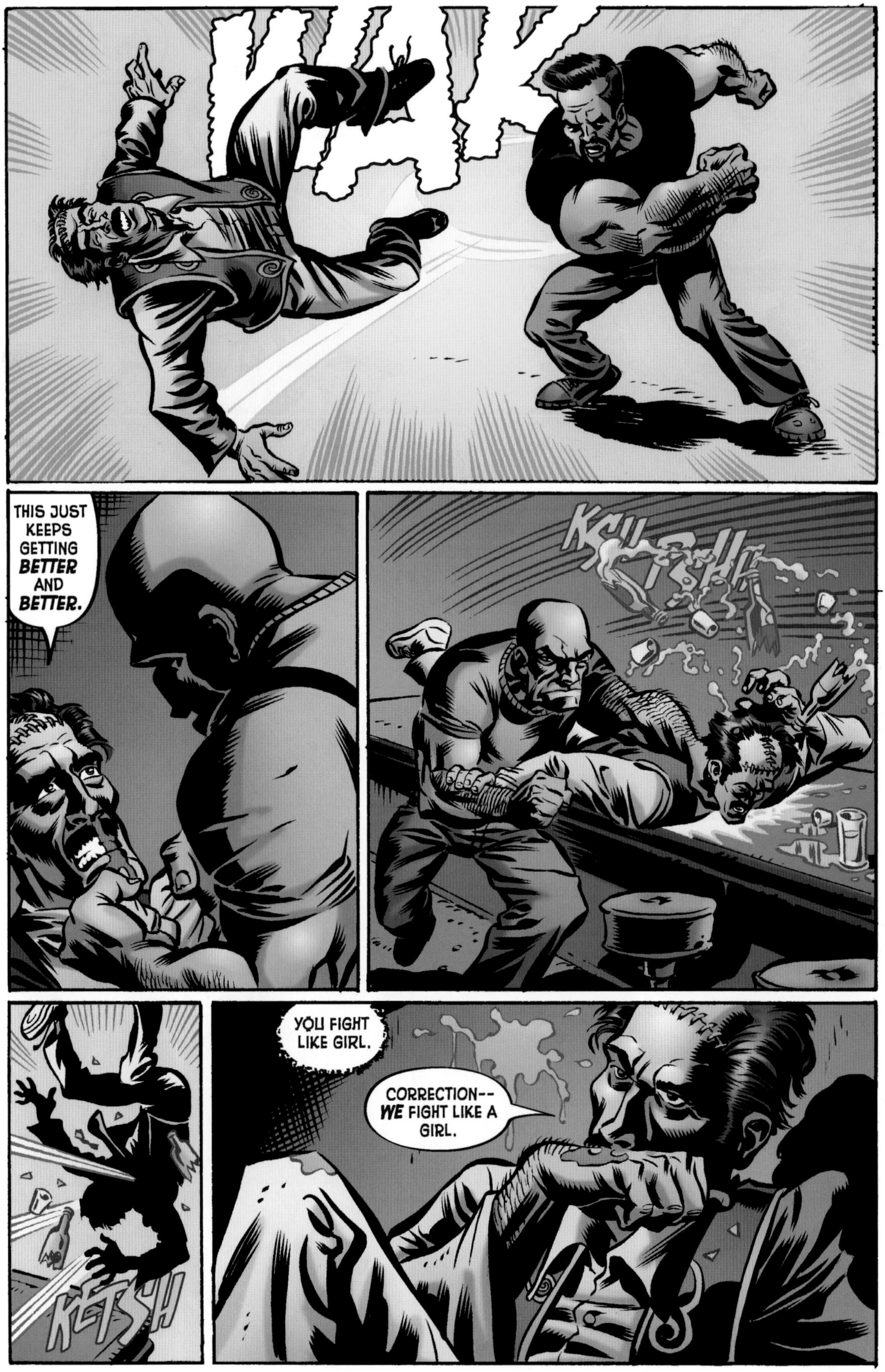
WAK
THIS JUST KEEPS GETTING BETTER AND BETTER.
KETSH
YOU FIGHT LIKE GIRL.
CORRECTION-- WE FIGHT LIKE A GIRL.

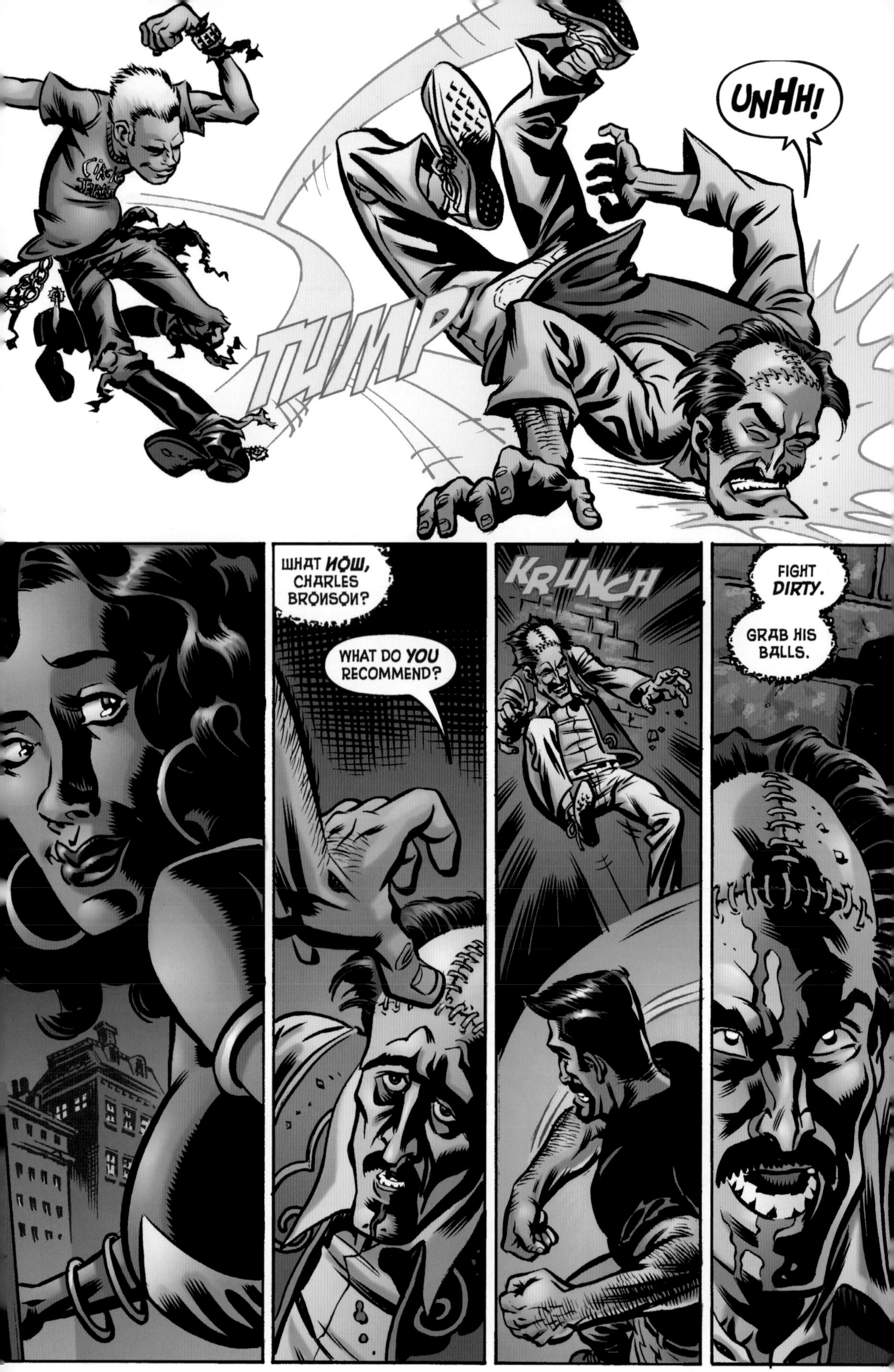
UNHH!
THUMP
WHAT NOW, CHARLES BRONSON?
WHAT DO YOU RECOMMEND?
KRUNCH
FIGHT DIRTY.
GRAB HIS BALLS.

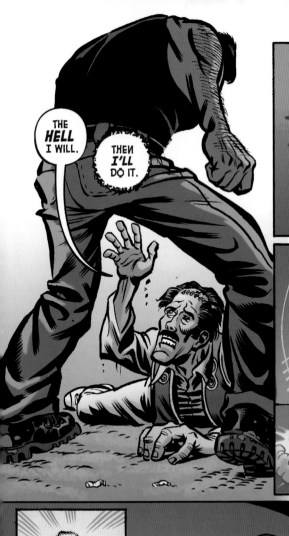

THE **HELL** I WILL.

THEN **I'LL** DO IT.

KRUK

THAT WAS **DISGUSTING.**

THUP

WUNK

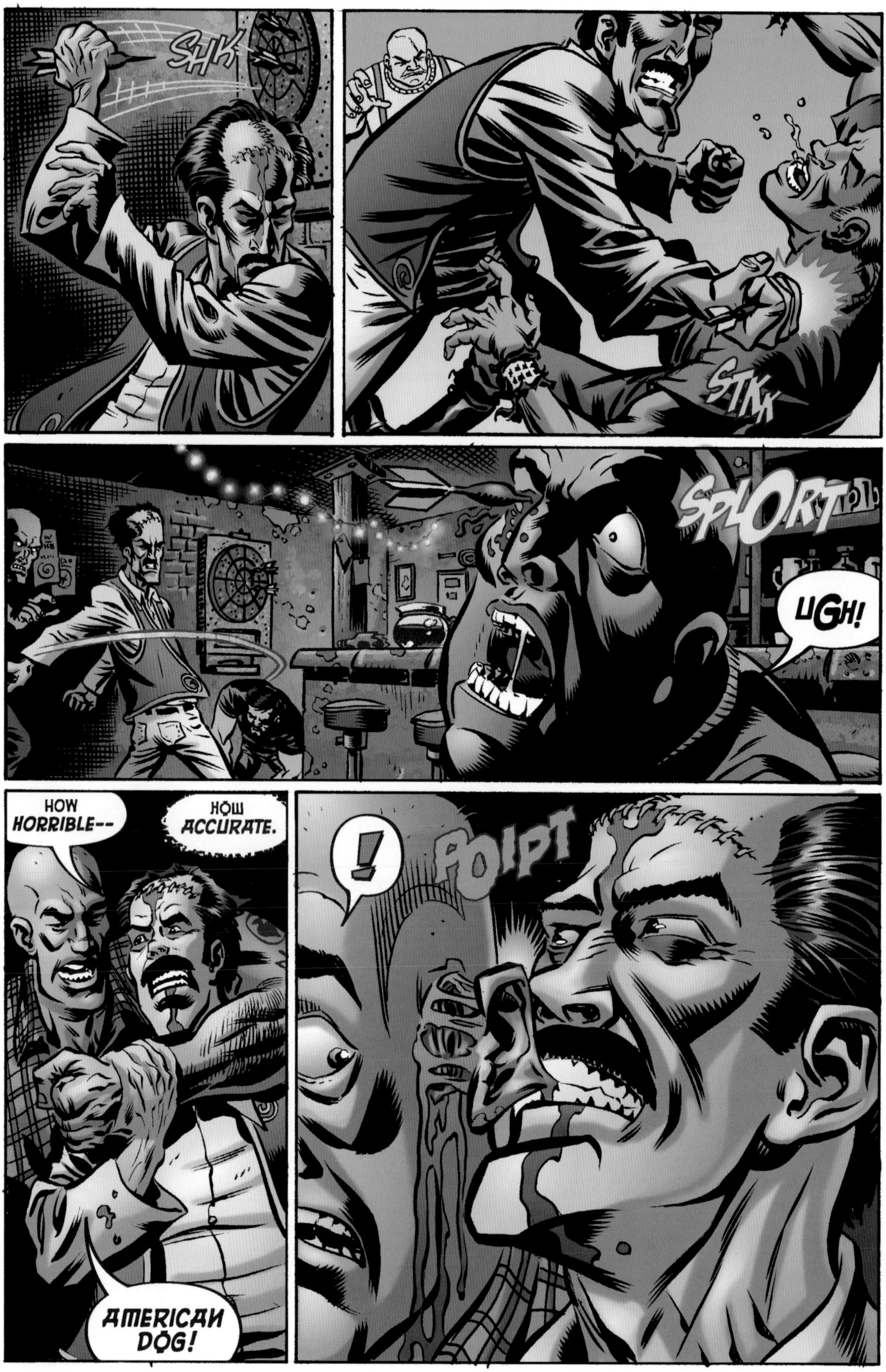
SHK
STKK
SPLORT
UGH!
HOW HORRIBLE--
HOW ACCURATE.
AMERICAN DOG!
!
POIPT

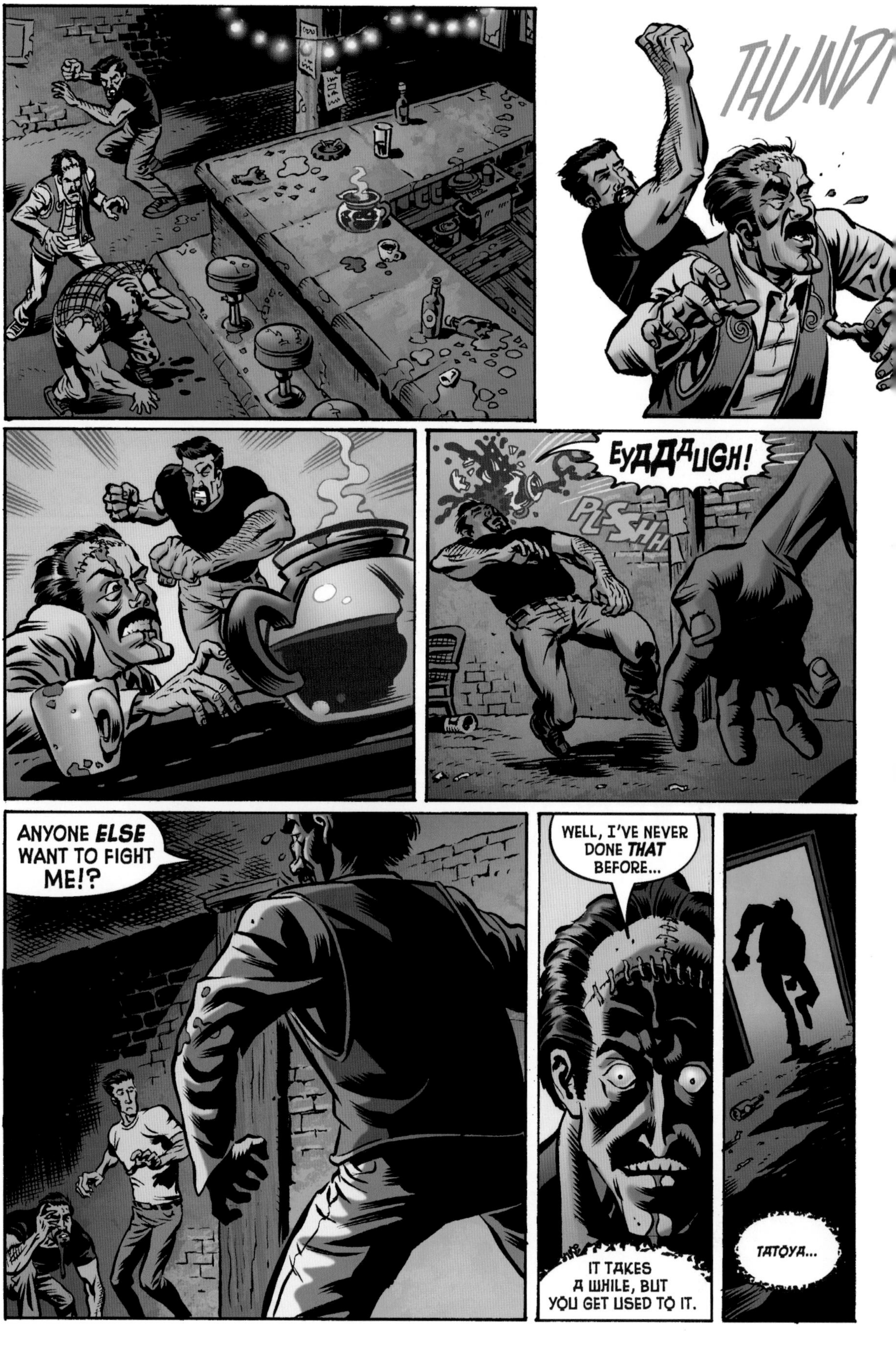
THUND
EyAAAUGH!
PLSHH
ANYONE ELSE WANT TO FIGHT ME!?
WELL, I'VE NEVER DONE THAT BEFORE...
IT TAKES A WHILE, BUT YOU GET USED TO IT.
TATOYA...

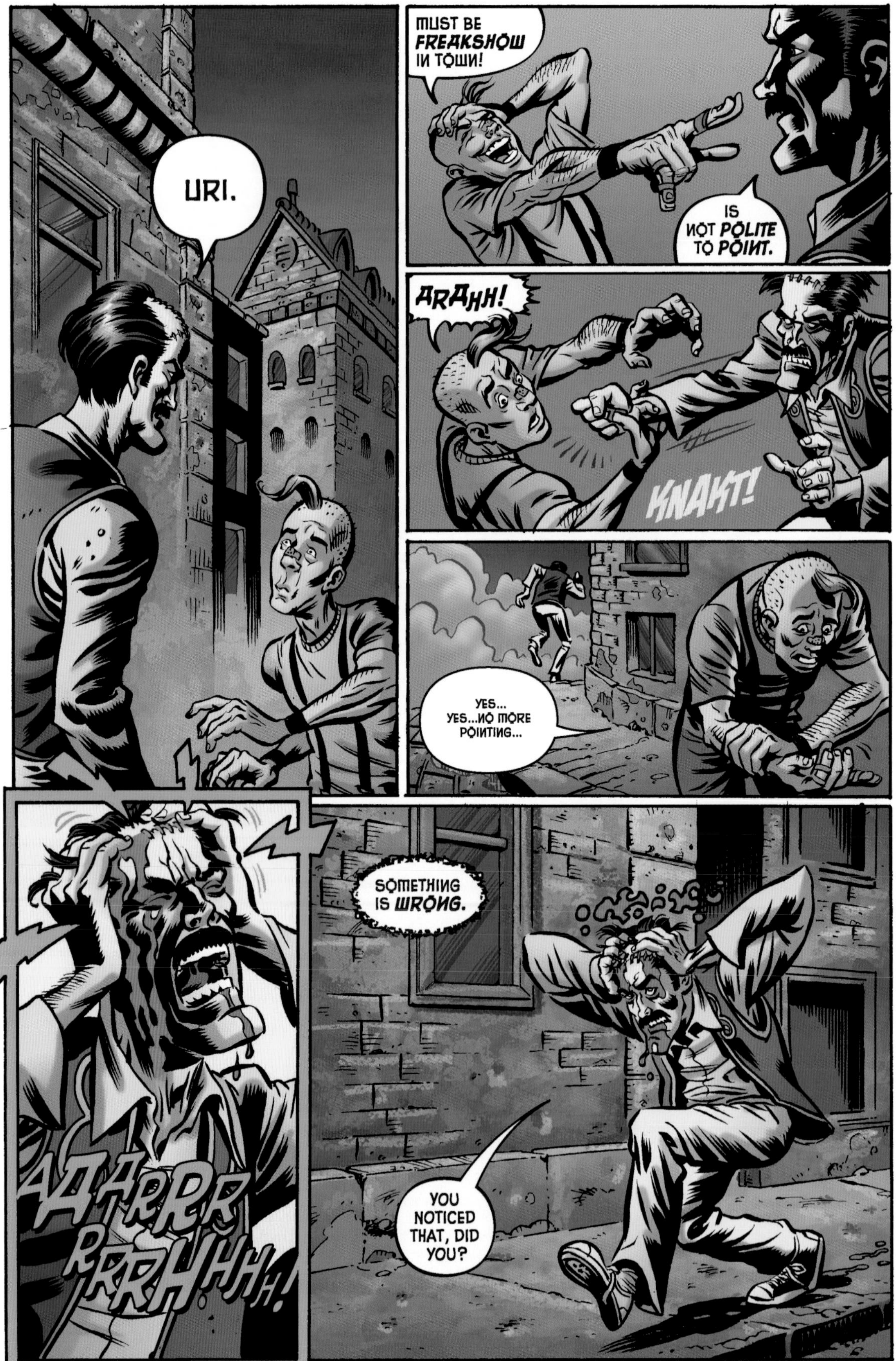

URI.
MUST BE FREAKSHOW IN TOWN!
IS NOT POLITE TO POINT.
ARAHH!
KNAKT!
YES... YES...NO MORE POINTING...
AAARRRRRRRHHHH!
SOMETHING IS WRONG.
YOU NOTICED THAT, DID YOU?

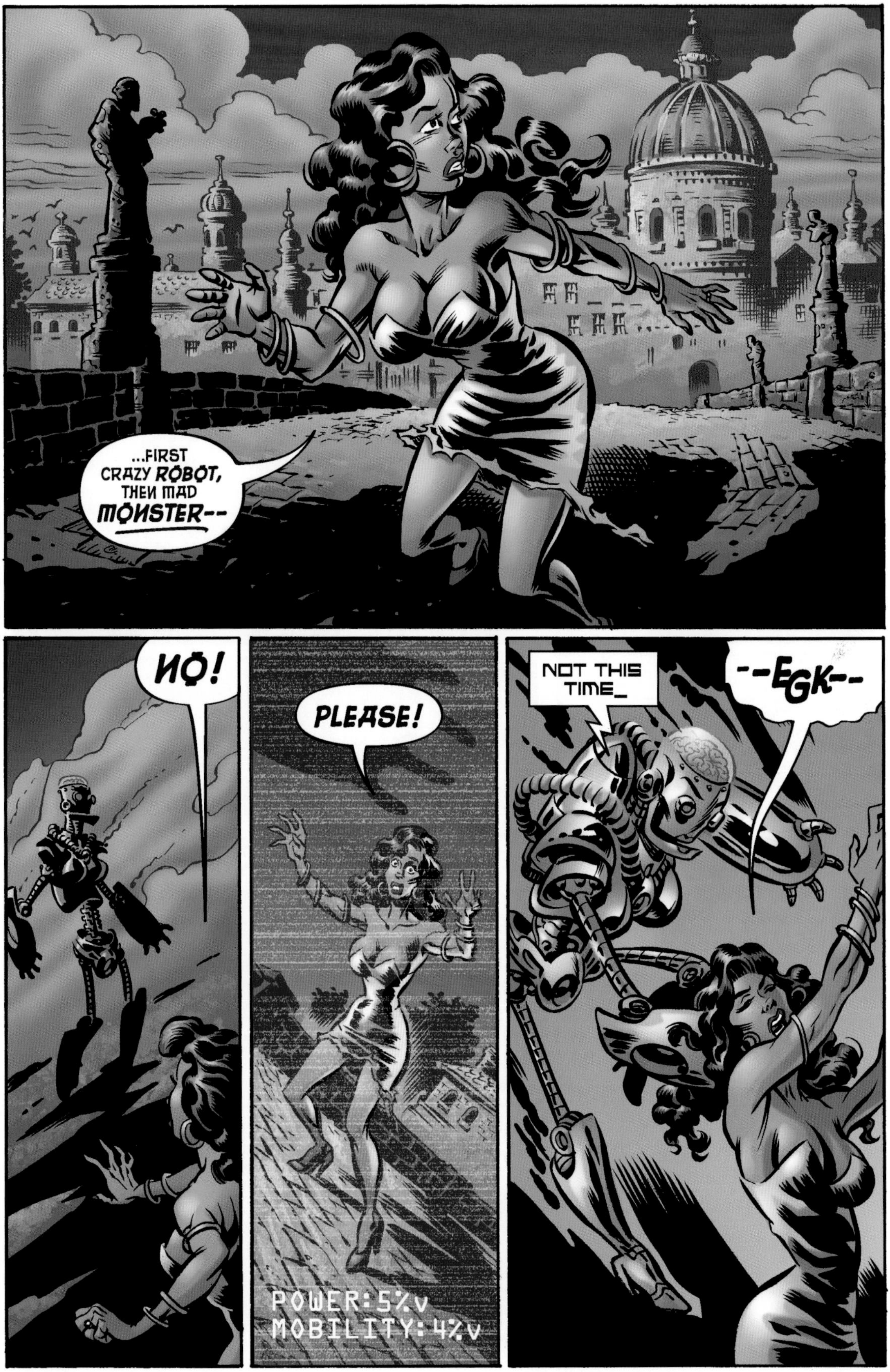
...FIRST CRAZY ROBOT, THEN MAD MONSTER--
NO!
PLEASE!
POWER:5%v
MOBILITY:4%v
NOT THIS TIME_
--EGK--

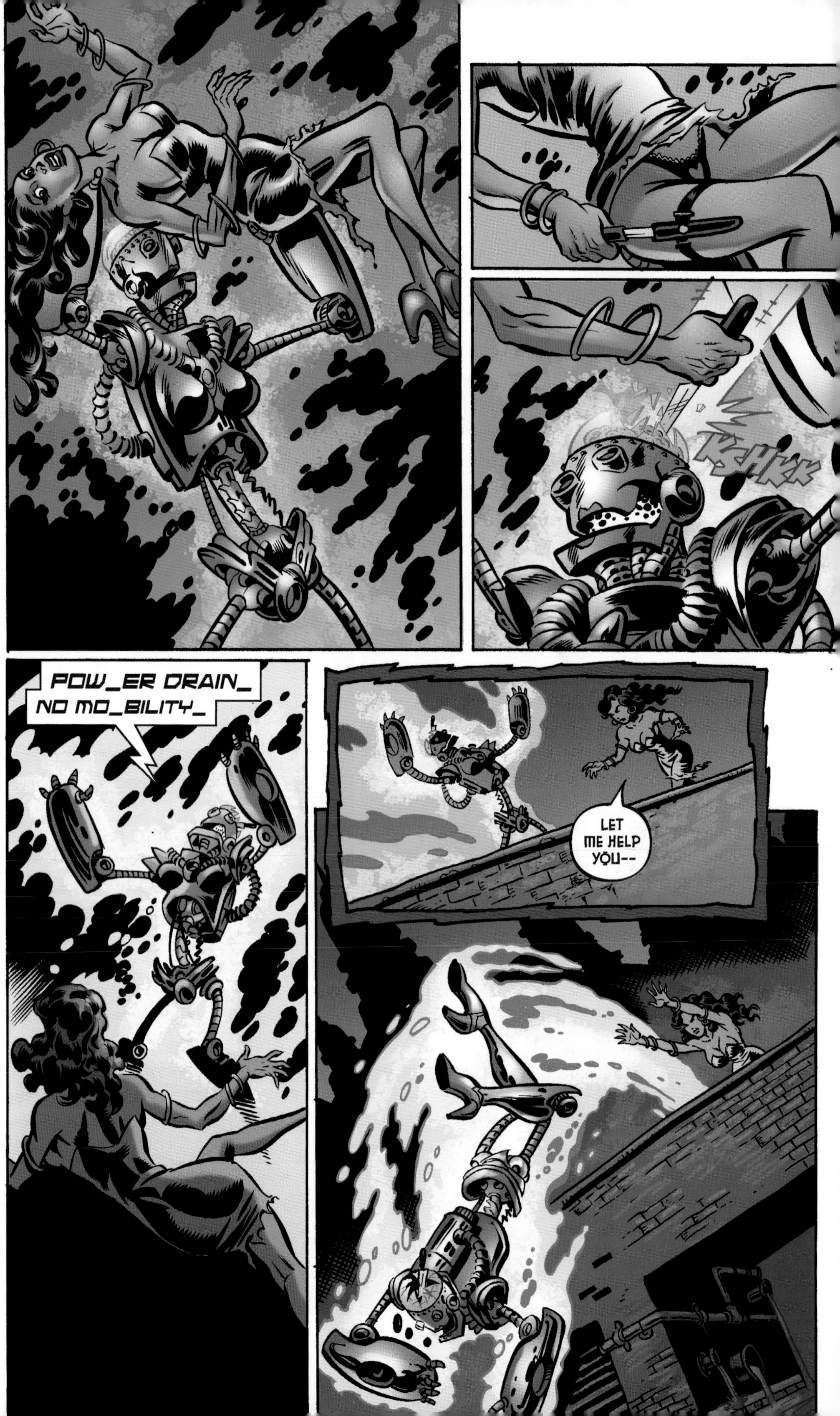
K-CHKK
POW_ER DRAIN_
NO MO_BILITY_
LET ME HELP YOU--

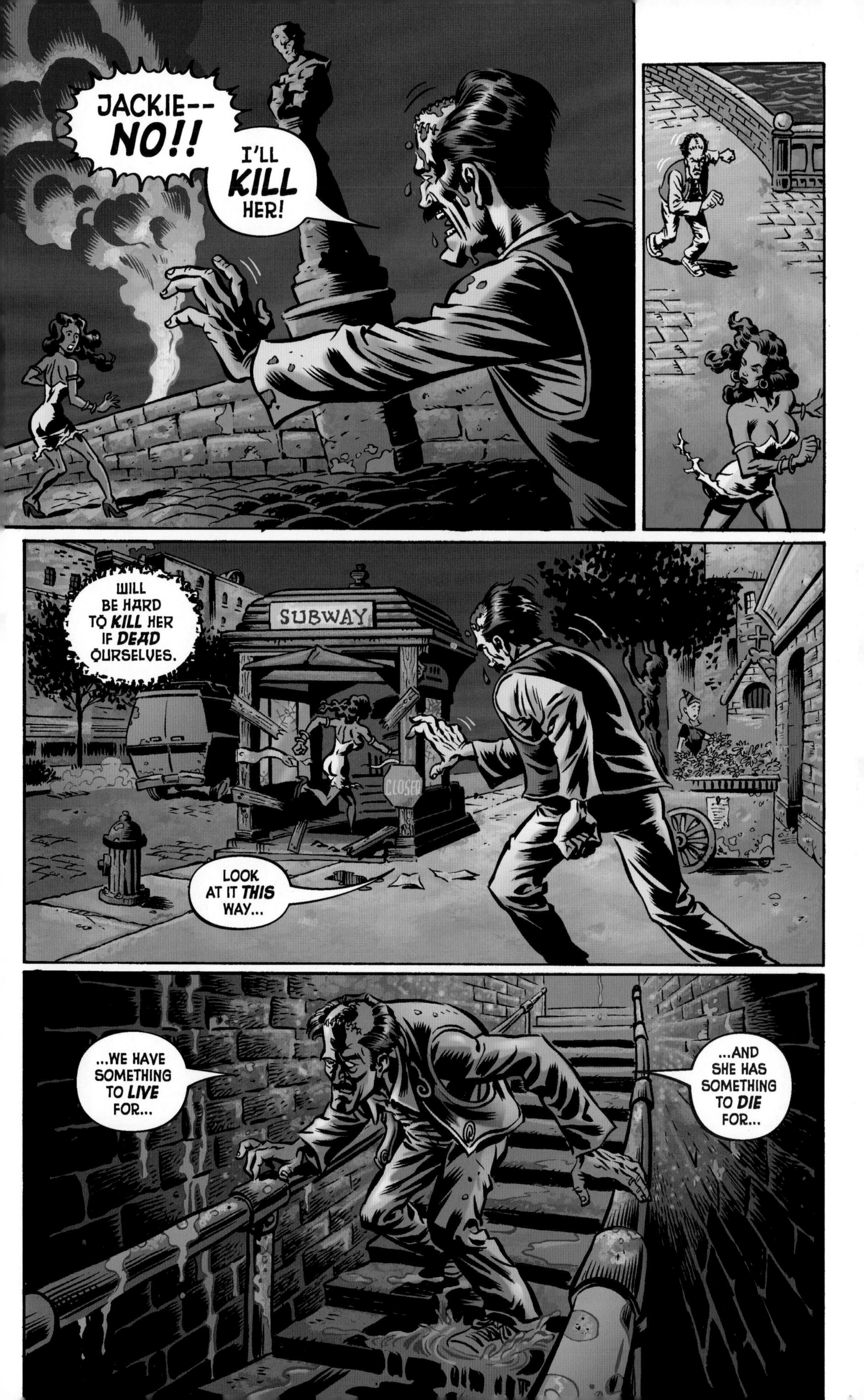
JACKIE-- NO!!
I'LL KILL HER!
WILL BE HARD TO KILL HER IF DEAD OURSELVES.
SUBWAY
CLOSED
LOOK AT IT THIS WAY...
...WE HAVE SOMETHING TO LIVE FOR...
...AND SHE HAS SOMETHING TO DIE FOR...

plip
plish

SRANK
SRANK
RANK

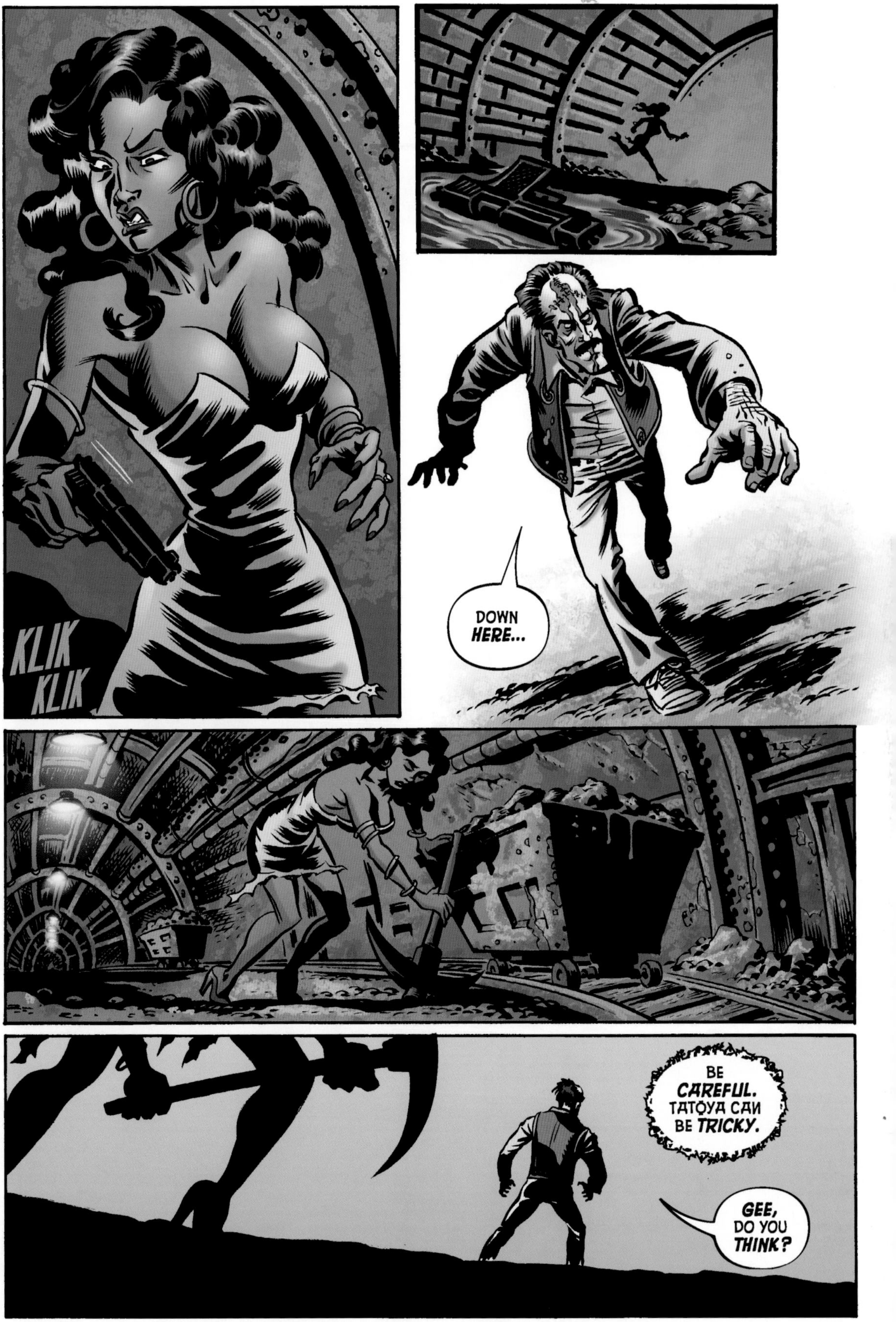
KLIK
KLIK
DOWN HERE...
BE CAREFUL. TATOYA CAN BE TRICKY.
GEE, DO YOU THINK?

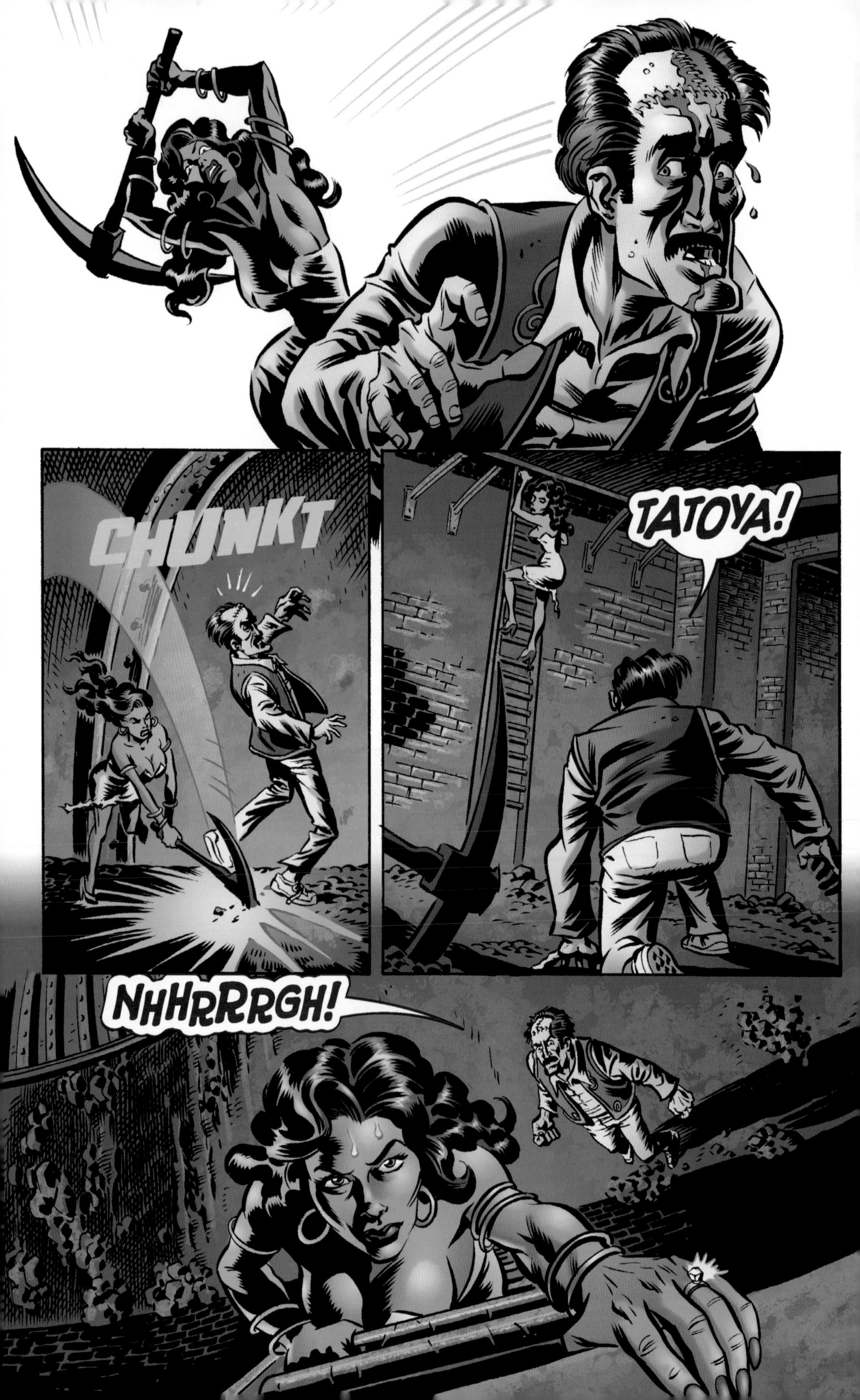
CHUNKT
TATOYA!
NHHRRRGH!

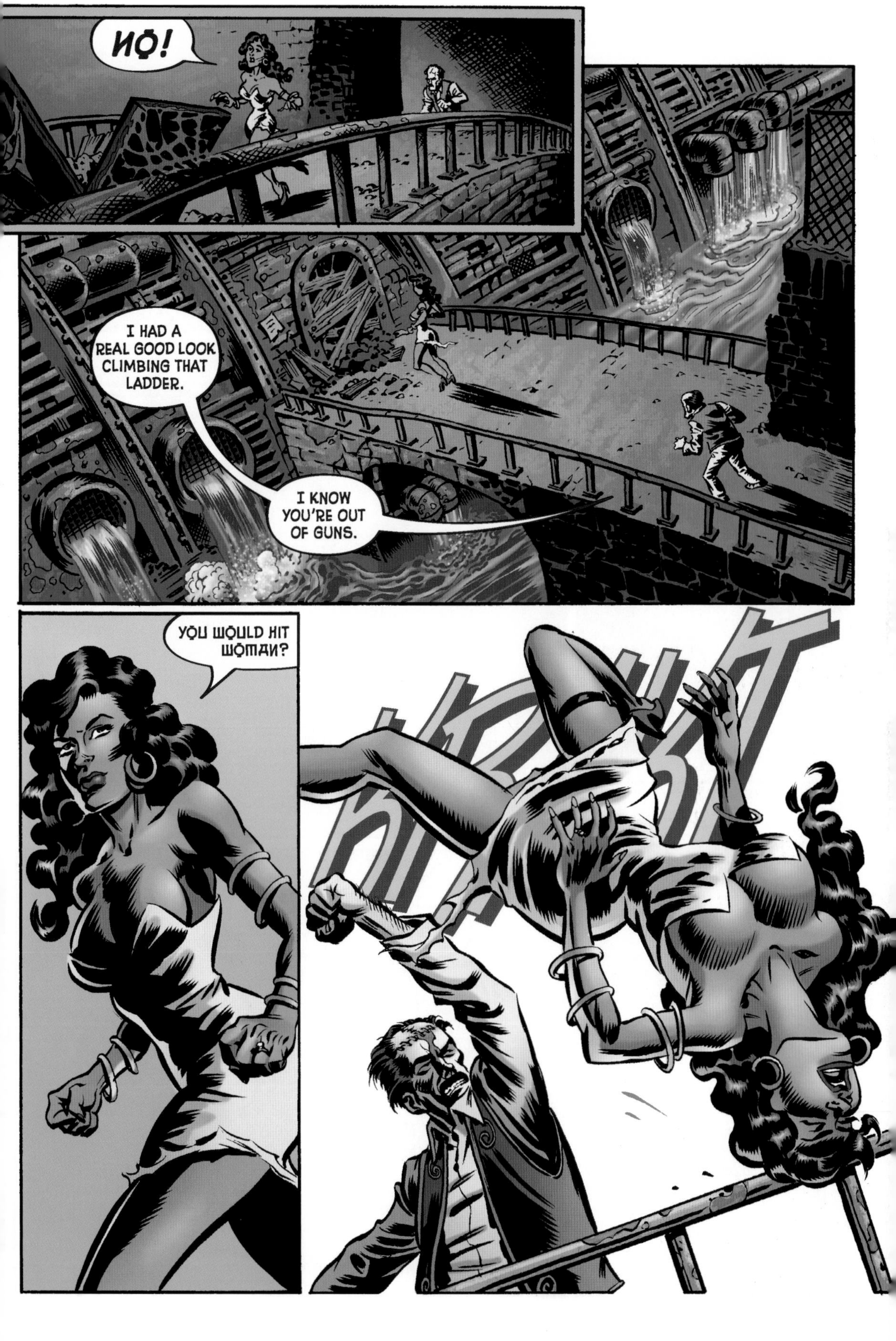
NO!
I HAD A REAL GOOD LOOK CLIMBING THAT LADDER.
I KNOW YOU'RE OUT OF GUNS.
YOU WOULD HIT WOMAN?

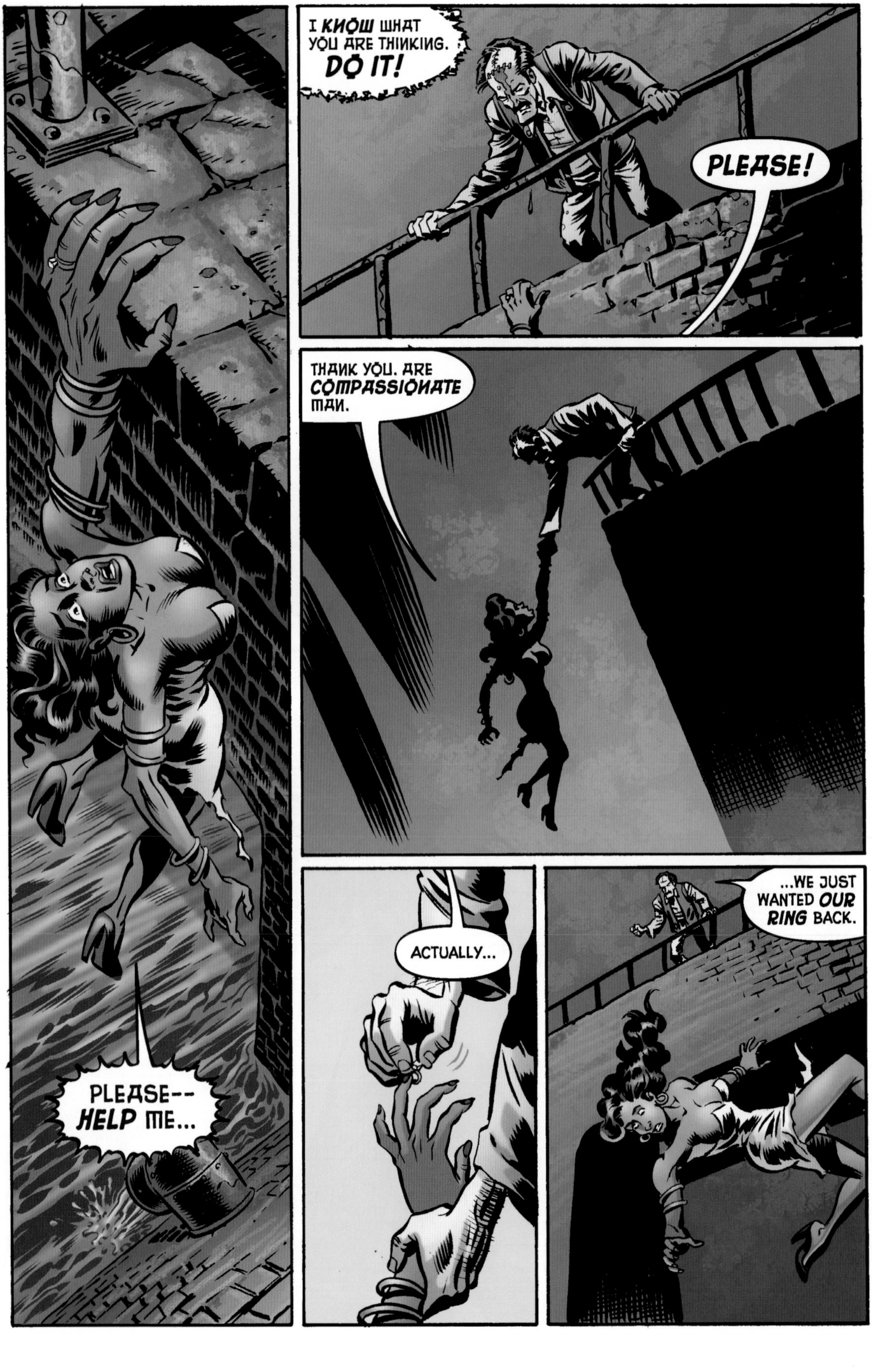
PLEASE--
HELP ME...
I KNOW WHAT YOU ARE THINKING. DO IT!
PLEASE!
THANK YOU. ARE COMPASSIONATE MAN.
ACTUALLY...
...WE JUST WANTED OUR RING BACK.

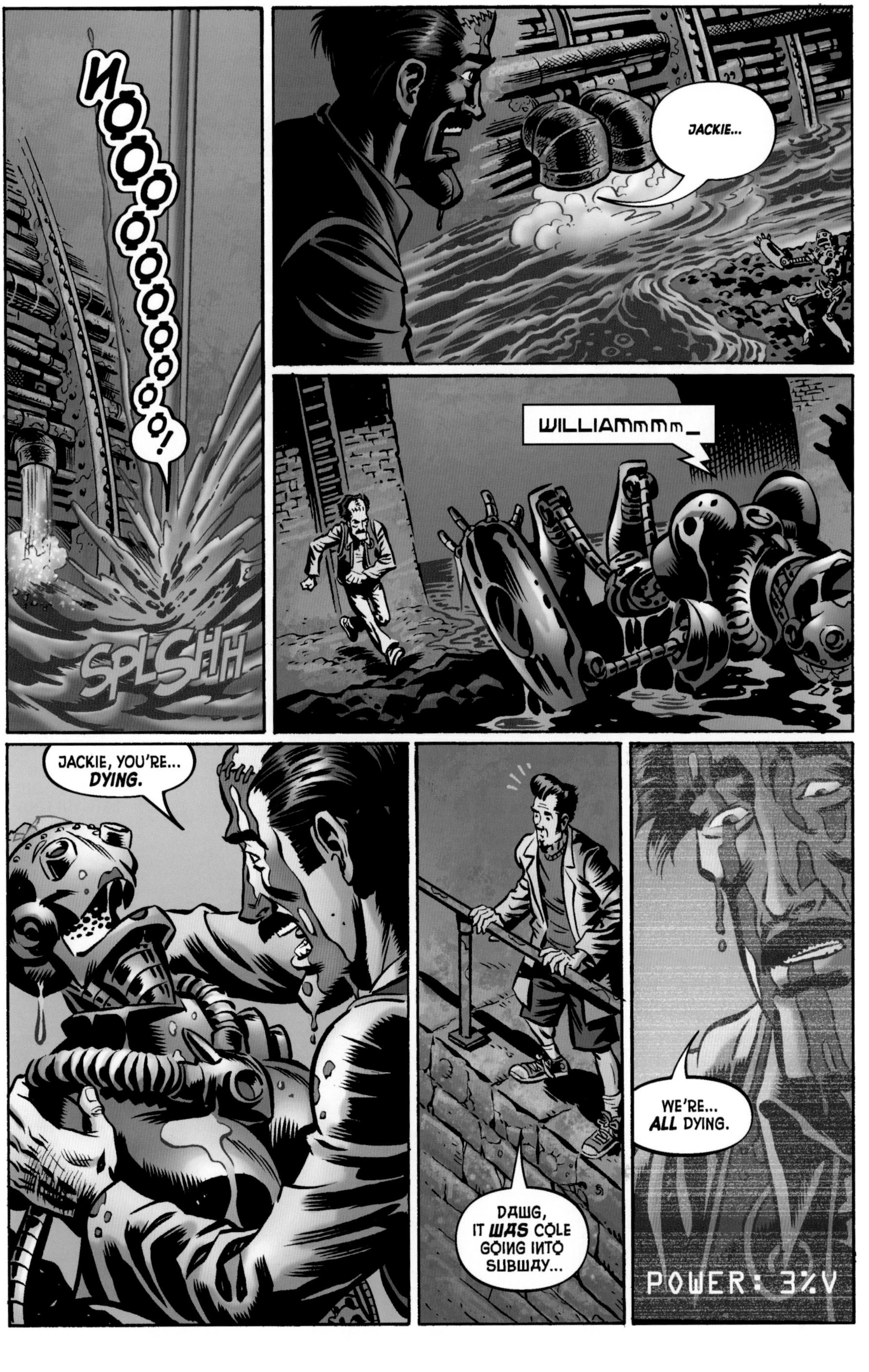
NOOOOOOOOOOOOO!
SPLSHH
JACKIE...
WILLIAMmmm_
JACKIE, YOU'RE... DYING.
DAWG, IT WAS COLE GOING INTO SUBWAY...
WE'RE... ALL DYING.
POWER: 3%V

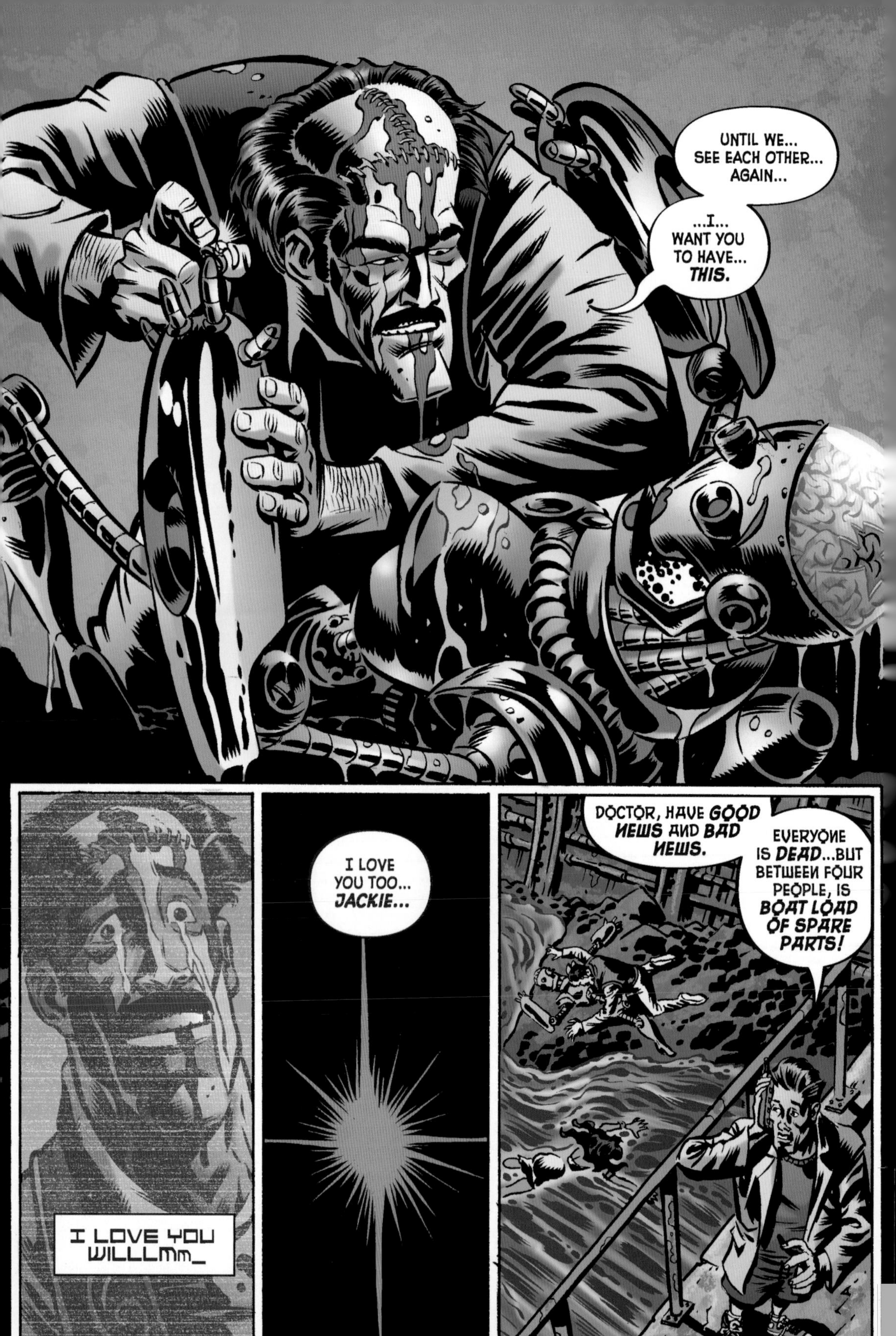
UNTIL WE... SEE EACH OTHER... AGAIN...
...I... WANT YOU TO HAVE... THIS.
I LOVE YOU WILLLMm_
POWER: 1%V
I LOVE YOU TOO... JACKIE...
DOCTOR, HAVE GOOD NEWS AND BAD NEWS.
EVERYONE IS DEAD...BUT BETWEEN FOUR PEOPLE, IS BOAT LOAD OF SPARE PARTS!

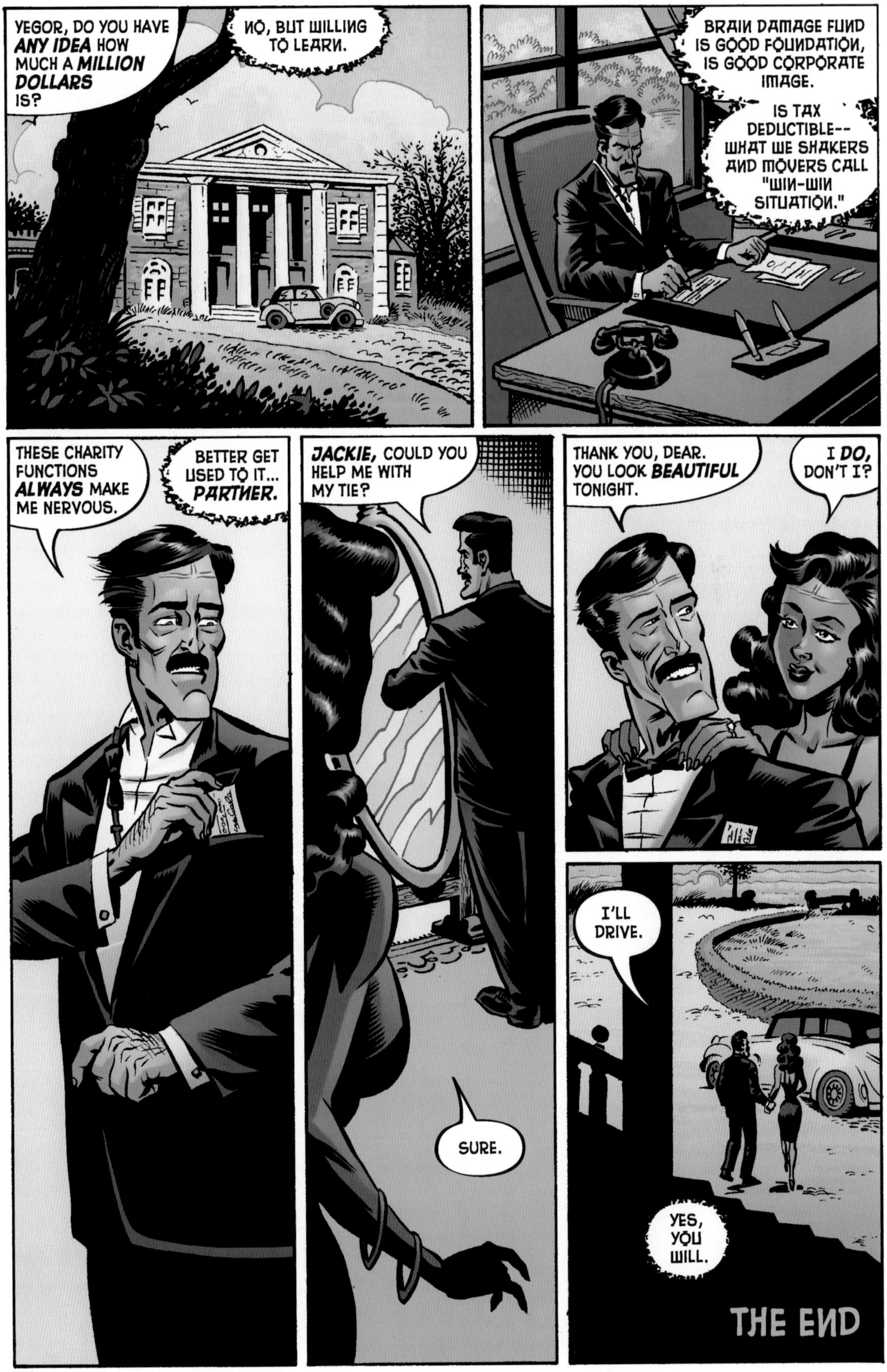
YEGOR, DO YOU HAVE ANY IDEA HOW MUCH A MILLION DOLLARS IS?
NO, BUT WILLING TO LEARN.
BRAIN DAMAGE FUND IS GOOD FOUNDATION, IS GOOD CORPORATE IMAGE.
IS TAX DEDUCTIBLE-- WHAT WE SHAKERS AND MOVERS CALL "WIN-WIN SITUATION."
THESE CHARITY FUNCTIONS ALWAYS MAKE ME NERVOUS.
BETTER GET USED TO IT... PARTNER.
JACKIE, COULD YOU HELP ME WITH MY TIE?
SURE.
THANK YOU, DEAR. YOU LOOK BEAUTIFUL TONIGHT.
I DO, DON'T I?
I'LL DRIVE.
YES, YOU WILL.
THE END

GALLERY OF THE

SCREAMING BRAIN ™

FEATURING

PHIL NOTO

HUMBERTO RAMOS
COLORED BY LEONARDO OLEA

ERIC POWELL

AND

MIKE MIGNOLA
COLORED BY DAVE STEWART

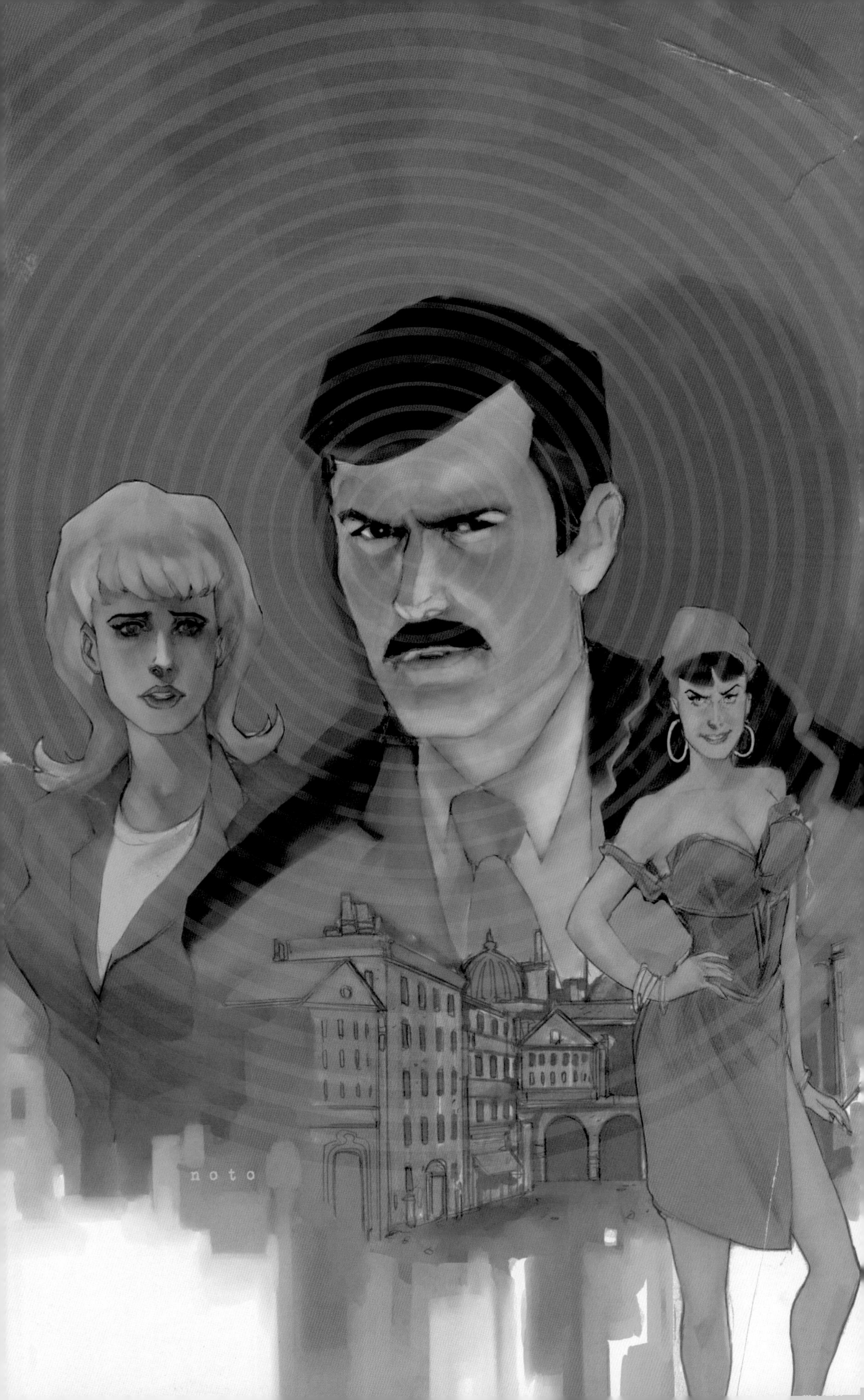
noto

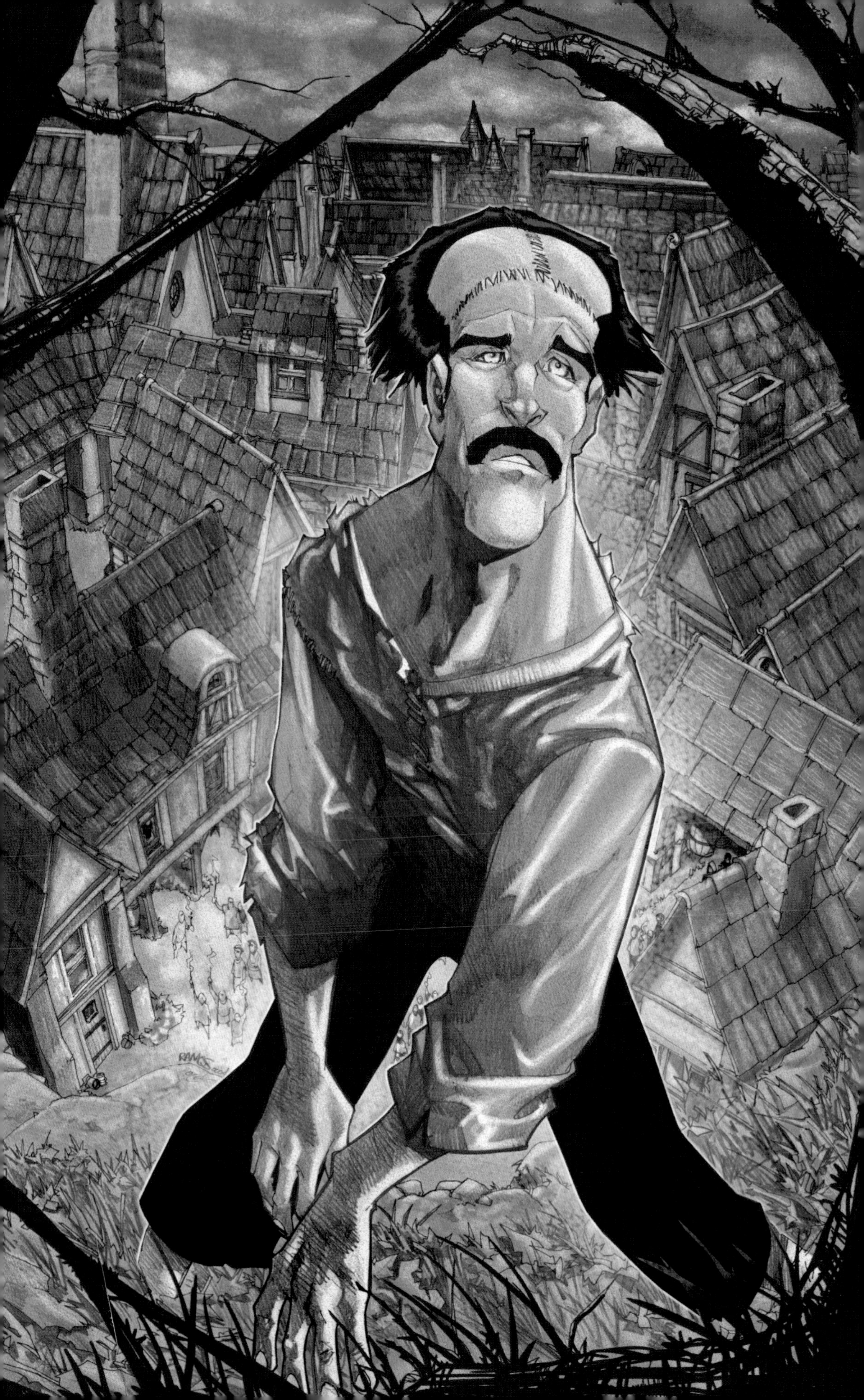

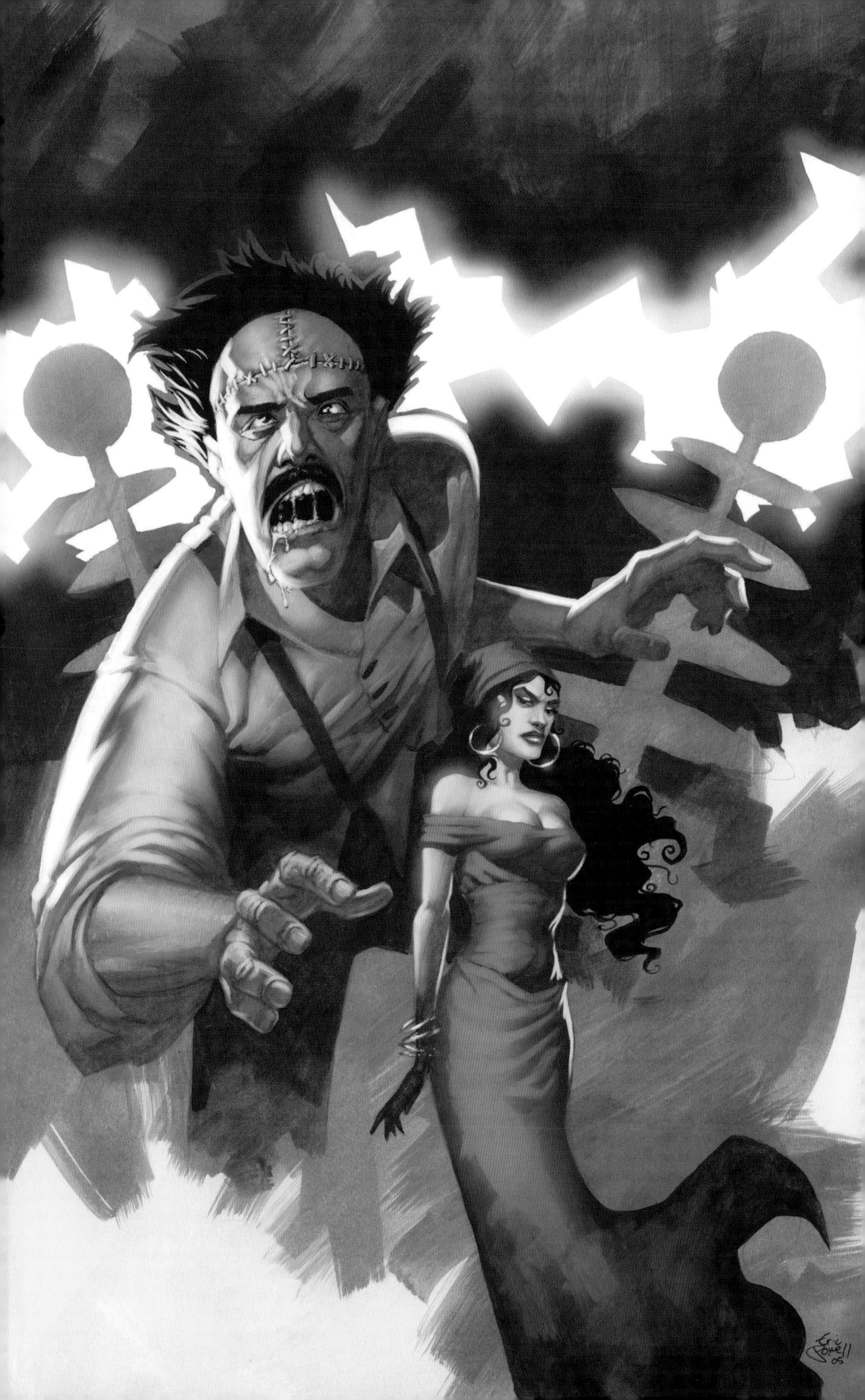
Eric Powell 05

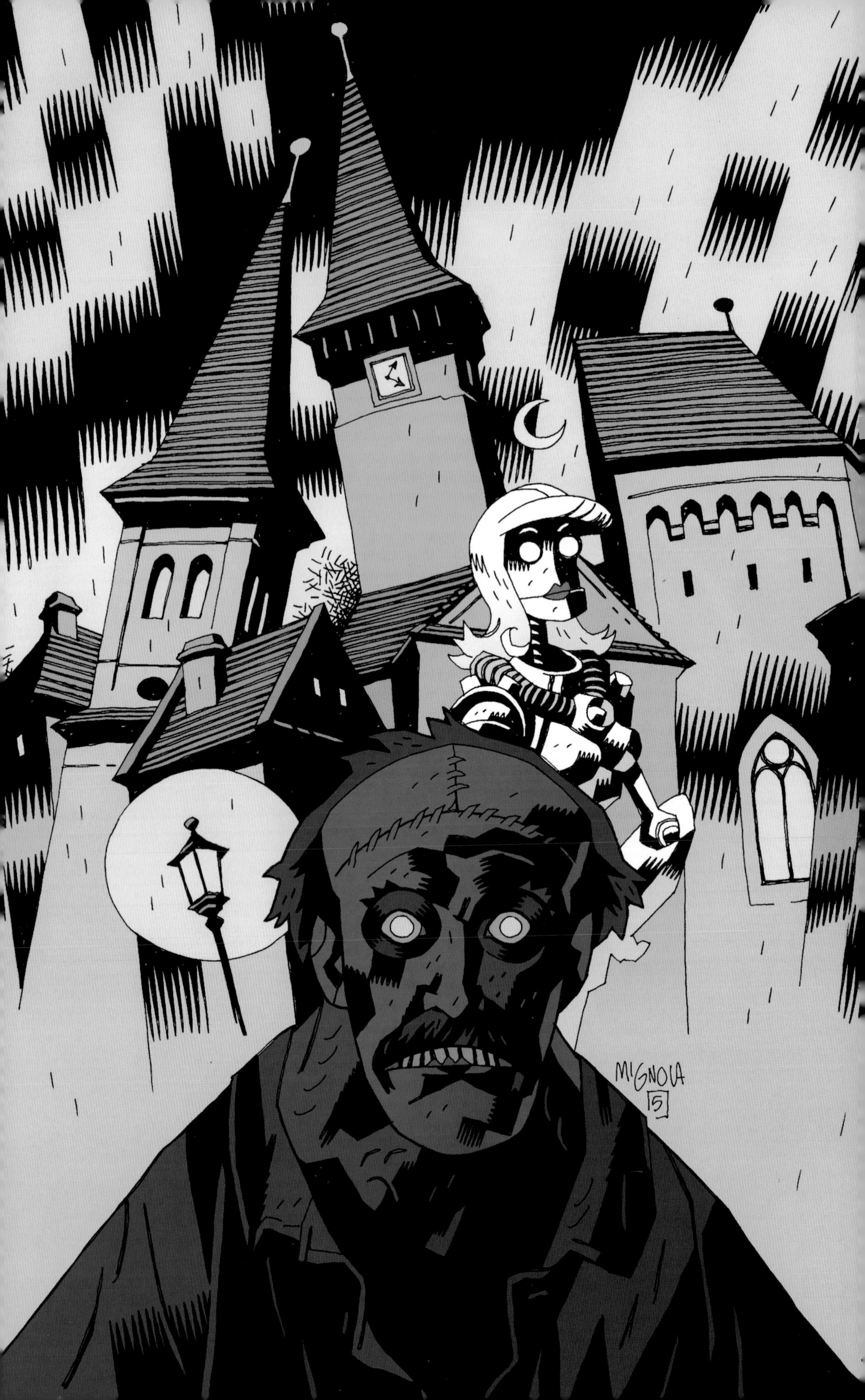
MIGNOLA
05

THE FOG

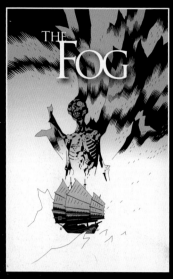

THE FOG

Scott Allie, Todd Herman, Andy Owens, and Dave Stewart. Cover by Mike Mignola

An ancient curse has followed a group of Shanghai traders to America. But what does this weird fog have to do with a pyromaniac refugee from the Civil War, or the terrible change coming over the Americans in this small seaside town? Filmmaker John Carpenter calls it "true to the terror of the film."

$6.95, ISBN: 1-59307-423-9

THE MILKMAN MURDERS
A MODERN SUBURBAN NIGHTMARE
JOE CASEY
STEVE PARKHOUSE

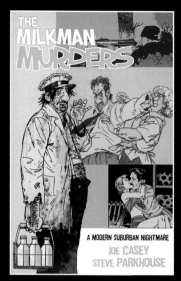

MILKMAN MURDERS

Joe Casey and Steve Parkhouse

After an assault by a mysterious and monstrous milkman, a typical American housewife has finally had too much of her hideous, deranged family, in this twisted parody of a Norman Rockwell image as painted by serial-killing folk-artist John Wayne Gacy. The shadows of the suburbs are darker than you could have ever imagined.

$12.95, ISBN: 1-59307-080-2

LAZARUS JACK

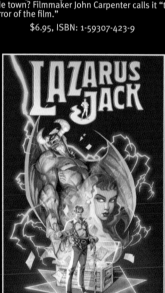

LAZARUS JACK

Mark Ricketts and Horacio Domingues

Escape artist Jackson Pierce made a deal with the devil that cost him his family. Now on a dimension-hopping mission to get them back, Jackson journeys through fantastic worlds and undergoes disturbing transformations, falling prey to an insane sorcerer, defying gravity, and ultimately confronting the demons of his own past.

$14.95, ISBN: 1-59307-097-7

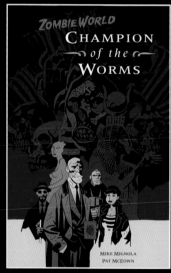

ZOMBIEWORLD
CHAMPION of the WORMS
MIKE MIGNOLA
PAT MCEOWN

ZOMBIEWORLD: CHAMPION OF THE WORMS

Mike Mignola and Pat McEown

A small-town museum is plagued by odd disturbances and missing persons—all part of the arcane work of their newest arrival, Azzul Gotha, a 42,000-year-old Hyperborean mummy bent upon sacrificing mankind to his ancient worm gods. Contains commentary by both Mignola and McEown and an all-new sketchbook section.

$8.95, ISBN: 1-59307-407-7

AVAILABLE AT YOUR LOCAL COMICS SHOP OR BOOKSTORE

To find a comics shop in your area, call 1-888-266-4226

For more information or to order direct visit darkhorse.com or call 1-800-862-0052 • Mon.-Sat. 9 A.M. to 5 P.M. Pacific Time.

***Prices and availability subject to change without notice**

DARK HORSE COMICS™ *drawing on your nightmares*

darkhorse.com